CONTENTS

02 FOREWORD

03 INTRODUCTION

04 ANATOMY OF A CV

10 ALTERNATIVE CVS
    10 Artists
    11 Film-makers
    11 Innovative approaches
    13 Electronic
    14 Academic
    16 Freelance & Self-Employed Creatives

17 CV CHECKLIST

18 CV EXAMPLES

44 MAKING CONTACT

46 COVER LETTER/EMAIL EXAMPLES

50 CREATING AN IMPRESSION

51 SHOWING YOUR WORK

55 REVIEWING PROGRESS

FOREWORD by Karen Millen OBE

© Rikard Österlund

In my work, I have read many CVs from students seeking work experience and employment. As an employer I have always tried to look at each CV, but it becomes clear very quickly which CVs catch the eye and begin to 'sell' a potential employee.

I look for specific information in a CV, such as experience, and an understanding of personal goals and achievements. I look for CVs that communicate quickly, that include something interesting about the applicant, and a CV that stands out. It is important to communicate both visually and with the written word in a professional presentation.

In today's competitive employment market, career planning should be embedded in education programmes. Students must learn to write CVs very early in their studies, which should evolve throughout their course. This Creative CV Guide sets out what should be in a CV and provides examples of how creative CVs might look from new graduates themselves. It suggests that CVs from graduates in the creative disciplines should be distinctive, and I would certainly encourage that.

With so much information available generally, it is fantastic to see a book that focuses on supporting students and graduates in the creative arts. I wish you all well in writing a CV and hope that it opens doors to your future successful careers.

Karen Millen OBE

INTRODUCTION

Emerging professionals have a hard time trying to get noticed amongst the sea of new graduates competing for those elusive and much sought-after jobs in the creative industries.

It is those emerging professionals, with whom I work, that have been the inspiration for the Creative CV Guide. As a careers adviser at a leading art and design university, I have taught and advised many thousands of students and new graduates over the years, as they travelled on their journey from inexperience and uncertainty to the confident and competent employees of the future.

Successful CVs and applications are all about understanding the target audience and being thorough and methodical in their implementation. Most people underestimate the amount of time and effort needed to create a CV that is right for its recipient. The reasons for sending the CV and the specific sector at which it is aimed, will help to determine its content, style and tone. The precise company and intended reader will further inform the detail, the content of the covering letter, choice of portfolio pieces and how to approach the organisation. It is this attention to detail that makes all the difference.

In order to help readers manoeuvre through this minefield, I have differentiated between types of CV and have created checklists that can be used at critical stages of the application process. A large part of the guide is given over to showing successful CVs and applications produced by students and new graduates.

This book is the direct descendant of a former book of the same name, written jointly by myself and David Whistance and published by the Surrey Institute of Art and Design*. Such was the popularity of the former guide that once past its "sell-by date" I was approached by several institutions about writing a new guide. What transpired was a consortium of three prominent art and design institutions: University for the Creative Arts, University of the Arts London and University College Falmouth. These three institutions worked together to bring the project to fruition and commissioned me to write this book. I am extremely grateful to them for their support and confidence to back this project.

The careers services of all three institutions have supplied the example CVs, cover letters, emails and websites included in the guide, and I am indebted to them and their students and graduates who agreed to show their work. Many of the CV examples have been selected by industry professionals, judging CV competitions within the three sponsoring institutions. My thanks to all involved.

Following on from the success of the original guide, the new publication builds on the strengths of its predecessor with new ideas and entirely new material. I believe we have produced an updated and comprehensive Guide for today's emerging professionals.

Jan Cole

Jan Cole

Jan has worked as a careers adviser for the past 16 years, after completing the Postgraduate Diploma in Vocational Guidance at the University of Reading. Having worked for several years in schools and colleges, she joined the Surrey Institute of Art and Design in 2000, where she managed the careers service whilst teaching and advising its students and new graduates.

In 2008, as a result of the high number of dyslexic students studying art and design, Jan completed a major research project 'Embracing Dyslexia, Creating Futures'. The study focused on the employability of dyslexic art and design graduates and contributed to her Masters in Guidance (Vocational/Educational) from the University of the West of England, Bristol.

* The Surrey Institute of Art and Design merged with the Kent Institute of Art and Design in August 2005 and is now the University for the Creative Arts.

ANATOMY OF A CV

INTRODUCTION

What is a CV, or 'Curriculum Vitae' to give it its full title? The phrase comes from the Latin 'currere', which means a course or career, and 'vitae' means life; so loosely translated, 'Curriculum Vitae' means 'course of life'. But this does not mean that CVs need to contain your full life history, for CVs have evolved over time. They are subject to fads and fashions, national and regional variations and sector preferences, and it is those sector preferences that are the subject of this book.

Contrary to popular belief, there is no such thing as a standard CV. The variety of examples in this guide reveal a range of approaches adopted by students and graduates emerging from creative courses within our universities.

Students and graduates seeking to establish themselves in the competitive world of the creative industries need to demonstrate a range of qualities and skills, if they are to stand out amongst the scores of applicants for every opportunity. The message will be conveyed not simply by words, but by the visual integrity of the document, by attention to detail and by originality.

Avoid CV wizards and prescribed templates. Your CV needs to be unique to you and to the person and organisation to which it is going. The exact content will depend on the purpose of the CV, the job specification or requirements, what you have to "sell" and how you want to present yourself.

The order in which information is displayed is flexible and should be used to emphasise your most valuable strengths. Placing an important section or fact higher in your CV ensures it is read sooner and will help to keep the reader's interest.

Below is the type of information you **might** put in your CV. It is important that these guidelines are adapted to suit your individual circumstances and that you use your judgement and creativity when deciding what to put in and what to leave out, as well as the order in which to position each section. (The content listed below is written in relation to a conventional CV used for most jobs, work placements and speculative job applications. Alternative CVs on page 10 provide more detailed advice on other types and styles).

CONTENT
PERSONAL DETAILS

Consider how you are going to display this important information. As a marketing document, your name and contact details should be prominent and easy to read. Keep to essential, relevant information and only include additional details such as age and nationality if you really consider they will add value. In most cases, employers will have a rough idea of your age, simply by looking at the dates of your compulsory education. Although there are a few legal exceptions, equality and diversity legislation in the UK preclude employers from taking account of age, gender and marital status when selecting candidates.

Details should include:
- Name
- Address
- Telephone number(s)
- Email
- Website address or URL of online portfolio

Your personal details could form a heading to your CV and the style may be replicated in other documents, such as letters, business cards and DVDs. Further information about branded stationery is given on page 50.

CATHERINE DOUGLAS
UNIVERSITY OF THE ARTS LONDON

PROFILE　　Although this is an entirely optional section, it has become increasingly popular with both employers and CV writers. Only three or four lines in length, this is, arguably, the most difficult section to write well, but when successful, can greatly enhance an application. As this is normally the first part of the CV to be read, it is essential to get it right if you are to avoid the shredder at the first hurdle.

The profile is an opportunity to write a short summary that will grab the attention of your reader. Strictly speaking, it should be written in the third person but without mentioning yourself by name.

Example:　Recent textiles graduate, specialising in...

It should be short and positive, outlining a few pertinent key strengths. The profile will introduce you (new graduate, textiles designer, etc), highlight particular skills, interests, experience or knowledge relevant to the position, and refer to what you are seeking (work placement or future career in television production). You should not write about anything in detail as further information will be provided within the body of your CV and covering correspondence. The art is in getting these points over in a meaningful and original way. Anyone who reads a large number of CVs will come across the same tired phrases time and time again and, as a result, the impact is lost.

QUALIFICATIONS　　List your qualifications and the educational establishment where you studied, in one section. They should be written in reverse chronological order (stating the most recent first) and include dates. Current and ongoing courses should also be listed.

The more recent the qualification, the more detail is needed. Your degree will be of greater interest to recruiters than your school examination results. It is not necessary to list every school examination taken, but simply summarise accomplishments by indicating the number of subjects and level achieved.

Example:　2000 - 2005　　The Park School, Twickenham, London
8 GCSEs A*- C

Additional relevant information about your degree may be included in this section, elsewhere in your CV or in your accompanying email or letter. This could include details of modules studied to emphasise the nature of your degree, the subject of your dissertation to show a particular area of interest, or details of live projects to demonstrate commercial experience.

EXPERT OPINION

Lydia Thornley

❝ I don't need a CV to feel fancy; the quicker I can get at the facts, the better. But it matters to me that a CV is well written with good spelling, punctuation and grammar. Even where these are a student's weak point, and they know it and have got the detail right by marshalling some help, this tells me a lot.

In contacting design practices, I think it's important that it's clear that they've done their homework and are interested in what the practice does. And that they've got a name: "Dear Sir or Madam" is obviously scattergun."

Lydia Thornley – Design Consultant

CONTENT
EMPLOYMENT/ EXPERIENCE

First and foremost, recruiters are interested in reading about relevant experience, including paid work, placements and freelance commissions. It is helpful to separate this experience from other employment. However, if you are fortunate enough to have a wealth of relevant experience, then separating placements from paid employment may be useful. Write entries in reverse chronological order.

Include:
- Start and end dates
- Name of organisation
- Position or role
- Brief outline of responsibilities, achievements and results (but don't repeat the same skills for each job)

As with everything on your CV, it is important that you provide strong evidence of your suitability for the position. This evidence can be drawn from work placements, full and part-time work, commissions and live projects. Also consider other areas of your life: for example, sporting achievements can demonstrate hard work, dedication and team work; or gap year travel may provide evidence of organisation skills, independence and problem solving. Be factual and positive, using action words such as "achieved", "successful", "completed". Write in a formal style, avoiding use of the word "I" e.g. "Successfully bid for ...", rather than "I successfully bid for ...".

Although it is often said that there must be evidence of continuous employment with no unexplained gaps, this does rather depend on the stage of your career and the nature or type of work undertaken. New graduates certainly do not need to list every single part-time job undertaken since leaving school. In selecting what to include consider relevance, length of service, and what it says about you.

SKILLS

It is surprising how often people forget to inform employers of the specific skills they have acquired that make them particularly suitable for a post. Although it is not essential to have a separate 'skills' section, include your skills somewhere in the CV.

If a separate section is used, group skills into broad areas such as creative, IT, and transferable or soft skills (e.g. communication and team work), be specific and provide evidence, where possible.

Example:
Communication Skills - Made presentations to tutor group, mentored first-year student, telephone negotiation with employer to initiate and organise work placement, completed 10,000 word dissertation.

EXPERT OPINION

Mat Heinl

66 Generally, typography makes a big difference. However, some studios will be more concerned than other agencies. We think sensitivity to typography and typesetting at the very least shows attention to detail and interest in a core element of graphic design. If a designer is not confident or interested in type, it's probably best to keep things simple and concentrate on the areas they are confident in."

Mat Heinl – Design Director, **Moving Brands**

MAREN HALLENGA
UNIVERSITY COLLEGE FALMOUTH

**ADDITIONAL TRAINING
OR SHORT COURSES**

These may be listed under Skills or may have a separate section. Write entries in reverse chronological order and indicate course provider, dates, duration and mode of study (full or part time, or evening class).

**ADDITIONAL
INFORMATION**

Feel free to include in your CV any other information that may be relevant and will help to promote you for the position. These may be written in a separate section or incorporated elsewhere. Items could include:

- Achievements, such as scholarships, sponsorship or awards, responsibilities or projects
- Exhibitions: indicate dates, venue, title
- Competitions: indicate date, venue, title, result
- Languages: indicate level of proficiency
- Full, clean driving licence

**INTERESTS AND
ACTIVITIES**

Although an optional section of the CV, your interests are an indication of your personality and help the reader form an opinion of what motivates you. It is easy in this section to either sound very ordinary or else to try too hard by stretching the truth – something that may come back to haunt you when you are quizzed at interview. Rather than just listing a few activities, try to add something that is memorable or interesting.

Example:
I am passionate about wildlife photography and have developed my own website to publish my photographs. Many of my photographs are taken on Westleigh Marshes, where I work as a volunteer on a conservation project.

REFERENCES

It is standard practice for employers to ask for the names of two referees when recruiting and may specify whether they would like an employer and a personal referee or leave the choice to you. If, on the other hand, you are sending your CV with a speculative application it is entirely optional whether you name referees at this point. Bear in mind that speculative CVs may be filed for future use and it could keep your options open to simply write "references available on request". As a matter of courtesy, always obtain the permission of referees before listing them and check which contact details they would like you to use.

WHAT TO LEAVE OUT

Two things that are usually better omitted from a CV:

Passport photograph - Although it may be normal practice in some countries to include a photograph of yourself, in the UK it is not necessary unless you are applying for an acting role. What is more, research has shown that including a self portrait is frequently viewed in a negative light. It's best to leave it out. You will be asked if it is needed.

'Curriculum Vitae' - Do not use the heading 'Curriculum Vitae' at the top of your CV. Although it used to be the convention 50 years ago, everyone these days knows what a CV looks like and it is simply stating the obvious.

TARGETED AND PERSONAL

It is estimated that you have about 30 seconds (or 90 words) to grab the reader's attention and convince them that your application is worthy of further scrutiny.

Your CV should be a unique marketing document that aims to communicate and promote your suitability for a **specific** position. This can only be done successfully if you first research thoroughly the job requirements so that you have a good understanding of the organisation, its ethos and values. You will then be able to present a convincing case as to why you should be selected for interview. Throw in something unique or impressive and you should be on your way to success. It is rather like answering an exam question. Your CV may look good and contain a lot of impressive information, but if it fails to tell the recipients what they want and need to know (i.e. answer their questions) it is unlikely to be successful.

If applying for an advertised position, the job specification or job requirements usually give a clear list of the qualifications, skills and achievements sought. Less formal adverts or speculative applications, on the other hand, may require greater scrutiny to successfully identify what an organisation is really seeking. In most cases it is not difficult to find the information you need but think beyond the position itself. Find out about:

- the organisation
- their markets (potential and actual)
- major projects (planned, current and completed)
- reputation
- key personnel
- ethos

Use the internet and don't be afraid to telephone the department – most people love talking about themselves and their accomplishments and you may even get some golden nuggets of information too.

Fully equipped with all these facts you now need to provide evidence that you have all the skills and experience desired by the organisation. Put yourself in the mindset of the recruiter who may receive 50 or more applications for one position. How do they whittle down the numbers to a manageable level? Usually this is done by marking applications against the listed criteria for the job, so anyone who does not provide clear evidence that they possess all the qualities required is unlikely to be shortlisted.

KEITH ZHENG
UNIVERSITY OF THE ARTS LONDON

PRESENTATION

The look and clarity of a CV are as important as the content, especially for anyone intending to work within the creative industries. Whether you decide to produce a CV in a conventional or creative format (see page 11) is a matter of personal preference and appropriateness. Whichever format you choose, your CV is likely to be viewed and judged by individuals who will be critical of your creative skills and expect a high standard of everything you produce.

Obviously the level and focus of expectation will depend, to a large extent, on the type of organisation and the position being sought. Evidence of good design would be expected from a graphic designer whereas very high standards and originality of the written content would be key qualities required from a journalist.

Whatever your discipline, your CV must look professional, have visual impact and be easy to read. The reader's eye needs to flow easily and logically from one section to the next. CVs should be one or two pages in length. Never one and a half or three quarters of a page, or it looks as though you have run out of things to write. Each section should be clear, concise and factual. Avoid long paragraphs and do not repeat information. Where possible, try not to have sections spread across more than one page.

The choice of font, coloured text and layout can hugely influence the style and tone of a document and that attention to detail should extend to the quality and colour of paper, quality of printing and even the precision of the folding and the writing on the envelope. For a creative CV, these may be essential elements of the final product and can influence your decision whether to send it by post or as an email attachment, where the printing would be in the hands of the recipient.

Consider its suitability for a given audience. What type of organisation are you sending it to? Look at their website and marketing material to get a feel for the type of CV that might be well received. As well as suiting the employer, your CV should be a reflection of your personality. It is essential that you feel comfortable with its style and content. If not, you may struggle at interview or find that you fail to live up to the expectations of the employer.

Finally, pay attention to every detail of your CV – spelling, grammar, content and presentation – they all need to be executed to the highest standard. Anything less and you may be wasting your time, as the employer might think that you could not really be bothered. CVs are not written under exam conditions and you should allow time to get it checked and receive feedback from more than one source.

EXPERT OPINION

Caroline de la Bedoyere

❝ We are quite happy to find out about someone from a good CV. In order of priority, we go on experience, degree, then interests. To be honest, we also talk to specialist agencies who deal with the publishing industry and quite a lot of people do free internships in order to get into publishing. Mostly we are just pleased if they have bothered to find out something about us – you would be amazed the number who don't even look at our website before coming for interview.

I would say to your candidates get computer experience because there are so few jobs that don't involve that."

Caroline de la Bedoyere - Director, **Searchpress**

ALTERNATIVE CVS

....

INTRODUCTION

In the previous section, 'Anatomy of a CV', I have outlined the general rules and conventions related to CVs, but CVs can take many forms and are used for many different purposes. I will now consider variations to the standard CV and when to use them. Unless otherwise stated, the rules of CV writing explained on pages 4 to 7, apply.

ARTISTS' CVS

Focusing solely on you as an artist, these CVs need to offer a clear explanation of your work or collection (within an Artist's Statement) and a précis on your relevant background information about your professional development. Good presentation is vital. Ensure categories are clearly marked. You may wish to present your CV in a booklet alongside images of your work.

USES

An artist's CV can be used when applying to or for:

- Exhibitions
- Galleries
- Funding
- Potential customers/commissioners
- Awards

- Competitions
- Agents
- Residences
- Special projects

WHAT TO INCLUDE
Personal details

See page 4 for an outline of personal details that need to be included. It is particularly important that readers have access to images of your work, so give details of your website or URL of your online portfolio. If you have an agent, their contact details should be prominent in this first section.

Artist's statement

Use simple language that is clear and easily understood by your audience to present a personal explanation of your art. Contrary to conventional CVs, an Artist's Statement should be written in the first person (using "I" statements).

Try not to use pretentious language, but rather entice your reader so they want to go on to see your art with greater understanding. As each statement is individual to the artist and a specific piece or collection, it would be a mistake to prescribe its content. The following questions may help you to consider how you can provide insight into your work:

- **Context**
  > What is the background to the piece?
  > Why did you create it?
  > What influenced your ideas?
  > Is it part of a body of work or were you developing a theme?

- **Meaning**
  > What are the key themes of your work?
  > What does it represent?
  > Does it reflect a philosophy or vision?

- **Process**
  > What was the creative process?
  > What materials did you use and why?
  > What skills and techniques did you use?

- **Development**
  > Do you intend developing your theme further?
  > What have you learnt from creating the work?
  > What are your personal reflections on the work?
  > What are your ambitions for the future?

WINCY YAU
UNIVERSITY OF THE ARTS LONDON

ARTISTS' CVS
(CONT.)

Additional information to be included will depend on your background, the purpose of the CV and the stage of your professional development. The following sections are suggestions that can be used as appropriate:

Exhibitions/shows/work in galleries
Give details of dates, name of exhibition, gallery and location.

Competitions/awards/scholarships
List your artistic achievements (successes and short-listings).

Collections/commissions/projects
Give dates, title of work, name of collection or project and location. Include details of any funding you secured. If work is owned by a private collector, you should obtain their permission before publishing their details.

Education and professional development
Only include your art education and relevant short courses – show dates, institutions, course title and qualification.

Art-related employment or placements
These could include residencies, lecturing engagements or gallery work. Also list relevant voluntary work.

Publications
List reviews and references to your work. Include date and name of publication, title of article and page number.

FILM-MAKERS

Adapt the conventional CV format shown on pages 4 to 7 to include:

- Your area of speciality (camera, sound, post-production, etc)
- Link to website or online portfolio (if you have one)
- Technical skills – what equipment can you use?
- Employment – only include relevant employment. It's accepted that freelance film-makers will have additional fill-in jobs, but companies don't usually want to hear all about them.
- Filmography – make a clear distinction between films made as part of your course and those made commercially or for other purposes
- Passport – if you are likely to be working overseas
- Driving licence and car ownership – if you will be needed for location work

INNOVATIVE APPROACHES

There is much debate about innovative CVs within the creative industries. For some, the more unusual the better, whilst others expect a CV to simply provide clear, written information, relying on the portfolio to evidence creative skills. This places applicants in a dilemma; send the wrong style of CV to a company and their chances are doomed. This is where that tried and tested method – research – can help. Look at the company website and marketing information. Does that give any clues? Do you have any contacts within the company that may be able to offer some light to your quandary? Who will be receiving your CV? If it is HR or the finance manager, will they be interested in a highly creative CV or would they prefer a simpler format? How about phoning or emailing the company to ask what type of CV they would prefer?

It is the really unusual or wacky CVs that are most at risk. People either love them or loathe them. When they hit the mark they are a great success and interviews follow, but the rest of the time they simply provide light entertainment in the design office before ending up in the bin.

REBECCA CROSBIE
UNIVERSITY FOR THE CREATIVE ARTS

INNOVATIVE APPROACHES
(CONT.)

On the other hand, the advantage of producing a creative CV is evident. If well executed it will create a positive and lasting impression and will make your CV stand out from the hundreds of others received by the recruiter. But whatever style of CV you produce – novelty, wacky or plain – it must look exceptionally good. Nothing less will do as it will be seen as testament to your abilities and application.

Creatives use image and innovation for a number of reasons, so it is worth considering your aims:

Portfolio taster
As well as making a CV look more attractive, images of work can be used to promote interest in your portfolio or showreel. These CVs are usually produced in a traditional format, with images carefully placed to provide interest.

It is important that you are selective in your choice of images. They need to be relevant to the organisation and job for which you are applying, of a size and definition that allows them to be seen clearly and of a standard that promotes your abilities and enhances your CV.

The relationship between written information, images and the amount of white space needs to be carefully balanced to ensure the images enhance and complement your CV, whilst still allowing space to include all the details needed.

Skills taster
You may wish to use your CV to showcase a particular skill – drawing, 3D design or even wit.

Good illustration skills are often showcased as background images to a CV or with hand-drawn or hand-written sections.

Packaging designers are particularly good at producing CVs wrapped around enticing morsels, such as chocolate bars and sweets, and using the information on the packaging to extol their virtues. Obviously there is direct relevance in these as they showcase packaging design skills alongside the CV.

Some of the most entertaining CVs are those which demonstrate a sense of humour or a clever strapline. The CV itself may look fairly conventional or may depict or take the form of its subject, such as taking the shape of a foot for a 'foot in the door' message. In all cases it is the quality of the finished article that is of paramount importance.

Originality
Unusual and highly original CVs are not uncommon articles in the in-trays of creative directors. But producing something that will impress this critical audience, convey the message succinctly and show relevance rather than just frivolity, can be quite a challenge. Highly original CVs are usually very expensive to produce, in both time and money. It is therefore vital that you thoroughly research your audience to ensure it will be well received and will hit just the right tone for its recipient.

PROS AND CONS OF INNOVATIVE CVS:

PROS	CONS
✔ Can make your CV stand out and get you noticed	✘ Expensive and time consuming to produce
✔ Can demonstrate skills needed for the job	✘ 3D CVs are difficult to post and file
✔ Provides an opportunity to showcase portfolio	✘ Needs to be appropriate for the recipient
✔ When successful can lead to interview	✘ The design may leave limited space for written data

EXPERT OPINION

Russell Saunders

" As you would expect, a design agency will receive many CVs every week from students from many different colleges and universities. Your CV not only has to stand out from other peers in your college or university, but from every single design student in the country.

It's not wrong to produce a well designed A4 CV, but it has to be well written, charming and inviting to read. It's a real shame when CVs are sent out looking like a modified CV template. As creatives, applicants need to challenge the concept of designing a CV in order to grab attention and use it as a mechanism to express their individual work, personality and passion for design. In short, it needs to talk directly to designers not bank mangers. It needs to get us excited about you and who you are and make us want to get you in to find out more."

Russell Saunders – Senior Designer, **GBH**

ELECTRONIC CVS

More and more people are presenting their CVs electronically, whether it is housed on a website, sent with an email or forms part of an interactive presentation on a DVD. Each of these present their own challenges.

WEBSITES
See page 53 for advice on including your CV on a website.

EMAILS
If you decide to send your CV as an email attachment, there are several issues that need to be considered:

Compatibility – Unfortunately there are so many types and versions of software, that you cannot always be certain that the recipient will be able to open your attachment easily. Further complications can arise with some programs that are not always compatible between Mac and PC.

Security – Consider how easy it would be for someone to change your CV, for whatever reason.

File size – If you use a sophisticated program or insert images, there could be a problem in sending or downloading. You can guarantee that you will not be flavour of the month if your email slows down the addressee's system – not a good start when you are trying to impress! In addition, large files may be undeliverable due to a firewall.

The solution
It is advisable to save attachments in a PDF format if you wish to ensure they are secure, will download easily and look as you intended.

ELECTRONIC CVS
(CONT.)

OTHER CONSIDERATIONS:

Printing – Once sent electronically, you lose all control of the final product and must accept that your CV may well be printed in monochrome and on flimsy paper, losing the effectiveness of your creativity.

Company preference – Some employers have a definite preference towards either electronic or printed CVs. If in doubt, check first.

Professional image – You are now launching yourself as a professional and need to create the right impression from the start. If your email address is not appropriate for business then this is the time to obtain a new account for your professional career.

MULTIMEDIA CVS

These are a great way of sending examples of work alongside your CV. See Showing Your Work (page 51). It is often useful to get the interest of the employer before sending expensive DVDs as unfortunately some companies get so inundated with DVDs they rarely open them.

EXPERT OPINION

Trevor Price

"I personally still like something tangible to hold and read in my own time and space. With e-folios and websites you have to be connected to the internet, so for me it's limiting. I also think from a CV I can gauge how good at typography and layout candidates are. With the web they are pretty standard templates."

Trevor Price MCSD – Creative Director, **Price Associates**

ACADEMIC CVS

These are often required when applying for academic jobs, postgraduate courses and research funding. Although slightly longer than conventional CVs, it is still essential to tailor the content to the position you are seeking. The suggestions below should be adapted to suit your individual experience and the job requirements.

WHAT TO INCLUDE:

✔ **Personal details**
(See page 4) Academic CVs include the university address (if this is appropriate) as well as home address.

✔ **Academic profile (optional)**
Outline research interests and relevant experience and skills.

✔ **Education**
Only include higher education and professional qualifications (such as teacher training). List any awards or scholarships won.

HEI SHING
UNIVERSITY OF THE ARTS LONDON

✔ **Research experience**

Show past, present and proposed research. Give details of your supervisor and any funding received. As this is being addressed to other academics, it is appropriate to use technical language relevant to your discipline, but it still needs to be clear and easy to read. Further information about research projects, such as short extracts, can be attached to the CV.

✔ **Publications**

Include journal articles, extracts, books or broadcast articles. Use Harvard referencing.

✔ **Professional development**

Only record relevant training and skill development, such as courses and conferences related to teaching, learning and research techniques on your specialist area.

✔ **Employment**

Only include relevant employment, such as teaching experience (both formal and informal) and project management.

✔ **Presentations**

List any occasions in which you have presented your research findings or spoken publicly about your area of study. Alternatively, this could be included in other sections.

✔ **Skills**

Rather than listing a wide range of soft skills, it is useful to identify relevant skills for the position sought. Consider your technical or specialist skills, research skills, IT and languages.

✔ **Professional membership**

List membership of professional bodies and learned societies.

✔ **References**

Normally two academic referees are given; a third referee may be requested.

TIPS

✔ Ensure you are up to date with issues currently being debated within higher education and your specialism.

✔ Highlight any relevant international experience.

✔ Ensure you are conversant with issues of quality assurance in teaching, learning and research.

✔ Gain experience of making funding applications or bid writing.

✔ Try to get articles published in reputable journals.

✔ Demonstrate your proven track record to successfully manage a project.

✔ Attend seminars and conferences to keep up to date and to promote your own research.

CVS FOR FREELANCE AND SELF-EMPLOYED CREATIVES

By Elaine Banham – Head of Creative Careers, **University of the Arts London**

If you are planning to join the ever-growing legion of freelance creatives, you will need a carefully designed CV that promotes your skill set to the relevant potential client.

Be clear that you are in business and what service you are offering. Your opening statement should encapsulate this as well as catch the reader's attention. You could headline achievements, recent job successes or relevant training. Keep it short and aimed at the person to whom you are writing.

Your contact information needs to stand out – make it easy for busy commissioning editors or studio managers to contact you, so supply clear mobile, email and web information.

It helps to summarise relevant skills and experience as well as promoting your capacity to deliver 'the job', whether it's an illustration, a fashion event, an article for a magazine or design work. Highlight or list creative or technical capabilities and demonstrate commercial understanding in a concise and accessible way. Too long and the reader loses interest, too short and you may be underselling yourself. This first point of contact needs to express how well you manage and organise your own business. Even if you are in the early stages of building your freelance career, your CV is an opportunity to show confident information handling, flexibility and reassurance alongside your skills and experience.

EXPERT OPINION

Alison Coward

❝ I recommend that students practice writing about the non-technical or non-creative skills that they have. This will be useful when applying for funding or a loan, as there is always a section where you will need to justify your ability to manage whatever it is that you're applying for. This might relate to past work you've done and experience, but should also include things such as communication skills and the networks you're involved in. Give the funders confidence that you can handle their money responsibly!"

Alison Coward – Lead Officer, **Enterprise Centre for the Creative Arts (2006 – 09)**

Stating your full degree and university alongside a brief outline of course content enables you to highlight your dissertation subject, how you organised your final show or worked on live briefs and won prizes. If you are just starting, this is an excellent way of relaying your accomplishments. You may also be writing to a fellow alumnus as networking is a constant if you are freelancing in the creative industries.

You will want to illustrate how you identified and solved problems and show how well you responded under pressure. You may be able to demonstrate your resourcefulness, and your ability to work to deadlines and within budget or that you are able to communicate effectively to a virtual team.

Finally, make sure you include samples of work as hard copies or attachments, as well as on your website. Ensure they are easy to find, perfectly produced and entirely appropriate to the company or individual you are approaching.

CV CHECKLIST

1. PREPARATION

✔ Research the industry thoroughly to find out usual structures, roles and salaries. Use professional association websites, trade papers, directories, careers websites, etc.

✔ Find out about working practices, valued skills and the software and equipment used within the profession.

✔ Speak with industry professionals to gain inside knowledge of the industry, the company and the department.

✔ Check out key markets, clients and projects, managed by the company and the individual with whom you might work.

✔ Find out about the key achievements of the company and the individuals with whom you would be working.

✔ Study the job specification or list of preferred competencies for the post. If this information has not been sent with the job details, don't be afraid to telephone the company to find out the essential and desired skills, knowledge and experience.

2. CONTENT

✔ Ensure your profile clearly shows that you have the key qualities for the job.

✔ Present the information clearly and concisely.

✔ Place sections that contain your strongest qualities before less impressive information.

✔ Write your CV in the third person. Avoid using "I" or referring to yourself by name.

✔ Write the Education and Employment sections in reverse chronological order.

✔ Check that you have not repeated information or included anything that is not relevant.

✔ Use correct industry terminology.

3. PRESENTATION

✔ Scrutinise your CV for spacing and layout inconsistencies.

✔ Choose a clear, attractive format that is appropriate for the organisation.

✔ Ensure the balance between text, images and white space are pleasing to the eye.

✔ Give careful consideration to the style, size and colour of font.

✔ If your CV is two pages, ensure there is consistency between them.

✔ Start the second page with a new section.

4. CHECK

✔ Check and double check for spelling, grammar and layout errors.

✔ Ask someone who is experienced at reading CVs to look critically at yours.

✔ Check that you have included evidence of all the qualities required by the organisation.

PETRA TAOUJNI
UNIVERSITY FOR THE CREATIVE ARTS

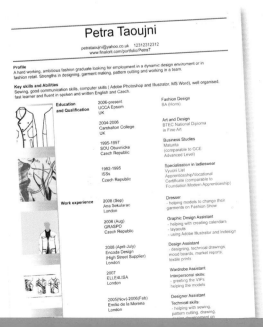

GRAPHIC DESIGN

CATHERINE DOUGLAS, UNIVERSITY OF THE ARTS LONDON

NEED A NEW FACE?*

* Inquisitive, quirky and conscientious Graphic Designer, complete with a range of placements under-belt, looking for a challenging, imaginitive and varied design agency with an interesting bunch of people to work with.

- Strong conceptual thinker, clear communicator, attention to detail.
- Good organisation, engages well in teamwork, efficient and helpful.
- Relishes learning through experience and observation.
- Enjoys print design, branding and ambient media.
- Proficient in Adobe Photoshop, Illustrator, InDesign, Quark Xpress, Word, Excel.
- Touch typing 90 words per min. Basics in Dreamweaver, Flash MX, Access.
- A person who considers creativity at the heart of everything, enjoys making bespoke pop-up cards and music and films that inspire thought and discussion.

EXPERIENCE

Feb - Mar 08: **Placement:** Publicis Hands-on Photoshop and design work on Wonderbra, Garnier, Oral B.
Oct - Dec 07: **Freelance:** SociaGuys Logo, literature and front-end design for a social networking website.
Placement: Black Dog Publishing General design assistant on publishing titles.
Oct 07: **Freelance:** Applied Information Group (AIG) Mapping and wayfinding signage for a pitch.
Jun 07: **Placement:** Big Fish PDF and packaging design mock-ups for Gü, Dorset Cereals
May - Jun 07: and Deliverance as well as assisting with pack shoots, competitor research.
Placement: Smith & Milton Work on concepts for CBRE annual report & branding.
Mar 07: **Freelance:** Viking Balcony Systems Corporate ID and literature.
Freelance: Silverstand Enterprises Carpet catalogue layout.
Feb 07: **Placement:** Billington Cartmell
Type, image editing and mock-ups for Dove pitch and Carlsberg, as well as
Aug 06: brainstorming concepts for Heinz, Côte d'Or, Ribena, Streetcar campaigns.
Award: 1st Prize D&AD Creative Award for the Parlophone brief
Jun 06: Engaging interactive masks designed for music festivals, encouraging creativity and fun, promoting talkability of Parlophone's artists.

EDUCATION

Oct 04 - Jul 06: **Chelsea College of Art & Design** BA Graphic Design.
Sep 02 - Jul 04: **Reigate School of Art & Design** HND Graphic Design.
Sep 01 - Jun 02: **Northbrook College** Foundation Art & Design.

TRY ME ON FOR SIZE!

For a new face print both sides, cut along the dotted lines, stick front to back then call **Catherine Douglas** on 07659 588 692 or email catherineljdouglas@hotmail.co.uk

GRAPHIC DESIGN

ROSIE UPRIGHT

http://rosieupright.blogspot.com
rosie.upright@yahoo.co.uk
12312312312 D.O.B 00.00.1986

 **Profile**

Designer and image maker.
Work focuses on the hand rendered, tactile and concept
based areas of visual communication.
Looking for employment and/or experience in the
Design Industry.

 **Education**

University for the Creative Arts at Epsom. 2006 - 2009
BA Hons Graphic Design (2.1)
Areas covered - Illustration, Typography, Packaging

Cleveland College of Art and Design. 2005 - 2006
Foundation Course (Merit)
AS Photography (A)

City of Sunderland College. 2003 - 2005
4 A levels Graphic Design (A) Theatre Studies (B)
English Language (B) Film Studies (C)

Monkwearmouth Comprehensive School. Sunderland. 1998 - 2003
11 GCSEs ranging from A*- C including Graphic Design (A)

 **Achievements
and Experience**

Collaborating with an MA Ethical Design student on final project, creating
illustrations and images for a range of cotton bags based on cotton production.
June 2009 - Present

Working with **Vaughan Oliver** designing the track listing for the Pixies
album, *Trompe Le Monde* as part of the reissued *Minotaur* box set.
February 2009 - Present

Work placement at **Delta Design Studio**, an independent book binders
based in Islington, London. February 2009

PaperCo Brief Encounters national competition. **Silver award.**
December 2008

Guildhall School of Music and Drama, examinations in Speech and Drama up
to Grade 5. Ranging from Distinction - Merit

 **Skills**

Extensive knowledge of InDesign Photoshop and Illustrator
and standard office applications. Comfortable with Mac and PC platforms.

Excellent group member, developed through three year role
as elected student representative for course and college committees.

Strong level of communication skills due to extensive drama training.

Proven time management and organisational abilities when meeting deadlines.

 **Interests**

When not disappearing under piles of paper, usually found reading,
collecting, visiting, photographing, walking, hoarding, drawing,
listening, spending, watching, talking and drinking tea.

References available on request

Gemma Willson

http://www.finalcrit.com/portfolio/gemmawillson, +44 (0) 7738294096
gembabe7@hotmail.com, 29 Orchard Way, Addlestone, Surrey, KT15 1LN

Well-presented, self- motivated, enthusiastic and creative individual. A reliable, responsible and flexible team worker. I have a friendly and open personality, enjoy challenge and acquisition of new skills. A graduate from Central St Martins I enjoy all things creative but especially Graphic Design & Animation . I find team work enjoyable and rewarding working within a group to create amazing results. Quite simply I'm an honest hard working designer looking to continue my career within the design industry.

SKILLS

Proficient in :

-Ilustrator
-Photoshop
-Flash
-2D Animation skills
-Office applications

Working knowledge:

-Indesign
-Dreamweaver
-Adobe Premiere Elements
-After Effects

Other Skills:

-Time management skills
-Meeting deadlines
-Team & interpersonal skills
-Communication
-Full UK driving license
- Over 21 years old

ACHIEVEMENTS
University of the Arts
CV Design Competiton 2008
I won second prize in a competition held by the University for the design of my CV.

WORK EXPERIENCE

Signco Ltd
Graphic Designer July 2008- Present.
Working in a small team.
Liaised with clients, learnt about
time management and deadlines.
As the only designer I have to manage
all design work, pre and post production.
Covering a whole range of products whilst
gaining new skills in Illustrator and Photoshop.

Boogles Ltd
Animator , *March 2008- Feb 2009*
Designed an animated Logo.
Also developing a short animation
to be used for a viral campaign.
Learning about working to a deadline,
time management skills and communication skills.

The National Gallery
Animator, *Feb 2007- Sept 2007*
Working with a brief from the National Gallery
I produced a one-minute animation based upon
one of their paintings. Learnt more skills in
Flash and time management.

Surrey Scout Association
Graphic Designer , *Nov 06 – Dec 06*
On a voluntary basis designed
an imaginative logo and learnt
how to communicate with the Client.

Thorne Creative
Graphic Designer, *Oct 05 – Nov 05*
Joint venture with a small group to design
a direct mail and website campaign for Virgin.
Learnt presentation and communication skills,
working to deadlines as well as working in a
small team.

EDUCATION

PgDip Character Animation
Central St Martins
October 2006 - June 2007

BA(Hons) Graphic Design
UCCA-Epsom
October 2003- June 2006

Foundation in Art & Design
UCCA-Farnham
Sep 2002 - June 2003

**A-Levels- Art,
Photography, Graphics**
Brooklands College
Sep 2000- June 2002

MY SPARE TIME

In my spare time I enjoy swimming,
visiting museums & theme parks
(Disneyland), photography.

I also like to read a variety of
fantasy and horror books.
I have taken part in Race for Life for
the last three years raising money
for Cancer Research, UK.

GRAPHIC DESIGN

Accomplishments:
- 5 years full time graphic design studio experience,
- Over 6 years experience working on a freelance basis for diverse, creative companies in the music, fashion and graphic design industries,
- Currently studying for an MA at CSM College of Art and Design,
- Achieved a 2:1 BA Hons Graphic Arts at Liverpool School of Art and Design in 2002.

Objectives:
- To work in a creative and challenging environment,
- To use my knowledge and skills to contribute towards the success of a dynamic, hard working design team,
- To be continually learning and developing new skills.

"At your service!"

CURRICULUM VITAE

June 2009
Current position
Full time student

FREE CUT OUT AND KEEP BUSINESS CARD!

CUT OUT AND STICK IN YOUR POCKET TODAY!
No obligation to call unless you wish! HURRY while stocks last!

Please write in BLOCK LETTERS below

NAME (Mrs / Miss)   Anne-Marie

HOME TELEPHONE NUMBER   01234567891

MOBILE TELEPHONE NUMBER   01234567891

E-MAIL ADDRESS   emailme@emailaddress.com

CALL NOW! FOR EXCLUSIVE OFFERS!!!

Cut along dotted line

PERSONAL DETAILS

Name: Miss Anne-Marie
Address: 1 Design Road, Designsville, UK
Home Tel: 01234567890
Mobile: 01234567890
E-mail: emailme@emailaddress.com
Status: Single
Nationality: British
Age: N/A
Date of Birth: 01/02/1903
Driver: Full, clean licence
General Health: Excellent, non-smoker

EDUCATION

SCHOOL / COLLEGE / UNIVERSITY		DATES		LEVEL	
Central St Martins College of Art and Design		2008 - 2009		MASTERS	
Liverpool School of Art and Design		1999 - 2002		DEGREE	
Manchester Metropolitan University		1998 - 1999		FOUNDATION	
Aquinas Sixth Form College, Designsville		1996 - 1998		'A'-LEVEL	
St. James' R.C. High School, Designsville		1991 - 1996		G.C.S.E	

We recommend using

iMac®

QUALIFICATIONS

LEVEL	SUBJECT AND GRADE
BA (Hons)	Graphic Arts (2:1)
BTEC NATIONAL DIPLOMA IN FOUNDATION STUDIES	Art and Design (Merit)
'A' - LEVEL	Art (A), Sociology (A), English Literature (C), General Studies
G.C.S.E.	Art (A), English Language (A), English Literature (A), History (A), Geography (A), French (A), Mathematics (B), Science (B), Religious Studies (B)

graphic design & illustration 2009 ©

1.

Continued Overleaf

ANNE-MARIE MOORE, UNIVERSITY OF THE ARTS LONDON

EMPLOYMENT

COMPANY	DATES	POSITION	PROJECTS
NATIONAL ARMY MUSEUM	04/07-07/08	Graphic Designer / Illustrator	Working alongside teachers and curators to create compelling exhibitions at the Museum. Producing gallery graphics from conception to completion, formulating solutions for the display of information, along with the design of various educational resources and publications.
JUNO	12/06 - 01/07	Freelance Illustrator	Illustrations for 'Favourite Worst Nightmare', the latest album by the ARCTIC MONKEYS
FINDEL EDUCATION LTD	06/03 - 04/07	Graphic Designer / Illustrator New Product Development	Designing innovative new products for Europe's leading educational suppliers. Work includes the design of various educational publications, furniture and fabrics, packaging, stationery, illustrations, branding solutions and the development of new teaching resources.
mercy	01/06 - present time	Freelance Illustrator	Illustrations for Liverpool based music / fashion / culture fanzine compiled by a collective of creative writers, designers and illustrators.
SAHMA &	06/02 - 07/04	Freelance Graphic Designer, Illustrator and Project Assistant	Working with young creative talents to develop artwork and branding for the promotion of music and dance performance events. Designs include brand identities, posters, CD covers, invitations and flyers for 'Urban Superstars' and 'Urbanize' workshops and competitions.
b-boi	06 - 07/03	Graphic Designer Freelance placement	Brand development and designs for children's printed clothing ranges.
Via COMMUNICATIONS	05/02	Graphic Designer and Gallery Assistant work placement	Creative graphic solutions for the launch of 'Urbis', including brand development and the design of merchandise for various clients. Designing window displays and assisting with visitors at 'Object 57'.

Proficient in: *(Please tick)*

Photoshop (CS3) ☑   Illustrator (CS3) ☑   InDesign (CS3) ☑   QuarkXpress 7 ☑

REFEREES

HOBBIES & INTERESTS

I ♥ music,

I ♥ reading,

I ♥ bands,

I ♥ to travel,

... and I ♥ to run everyday

Additional training 2007:
Advanced Microsoft Word,
Excel,
Powerpoint
&
Entourage

TRAINING CERTIFICATES

Miss Organised
Studio Manager, Design Company
Design Company, PO Box 123, 1 Design Way,
Designsville, UK
Tel: 0123 456 7890

Mr Tutor
Lecturer in Graphic Arts, School of Art
Designsville School of Art, 1 Design Avenue,
Designsville, UK
Tel: 0123 456 7890

Adobe InDesign CS3 Training Certificate, 17-18/12/07
Design Solutions, Designsville, UK
Adobe Creative Suite 2 Training Certificate, 2-3/05/06
QuarkXpress 6.5 Training Certificate, 05/05/06
QuarkXpress 7 - Software Upgrade Training, 20/10/06
Mac Digital Training, Designsville, UK

"At your service!"

Anne-Marie

2.

MEDIA

LOUIS CLAYDON

SUPERPH🎧NO🎧

MOVING IMAGE SPECIALIST WITH A PASSION FOR ADVERTISING

www.superphono.co.uk
louisclaydon@gmail.com
+44 (0) 7963789268

Education and Experience

National Diploma in Media Production - 3 Distinctions   NWHC, London Road, Hinckley, LE10 1HQ - 02/10/04 - 10/06/06

Bachelor's Degree at University College Falmouth   UCF, Tremough Campus, Treleiver Road, Penryn, TR10 9EZ

May 09

Roles: Event's Promoter   Advertiser   V.J   Cinematographer

Joint event organiser for a Superphono launch party hosting 150 guest's, working alongside V.I artist's to produce a live cinema experience of the Superphono showreel.

Technical experience: Resolume   Modul 8   After Effect's

March 09

Roles: Graphical Editor   Producer   Cinematograhper

A short viral campaign advert set in the city of Lyon, France, using a low grade filming format: the Kodak 7D710 SLR, to symbolise the French new wave "Point and Shoot" filming style.

Technical experience: After Effect's   Final Cut Pro

December 08

Roles: Media Campaigner   Web Design   Researcher

Working independantly I have provided an online hand book for young people living with type one diabetes: using my knowledge and experience of the condition to help to improve the individual's lifestyle. The handbook has been published by the NHS website and is available thoughout the country.

Technical experience: Dreamweaver   Photo Shop

March 05

Roles: Graphical Editor

Part of a thirty man production team to deliver a documentary following the Bauhaus art movement. The Filming of the documentary took place in New York, Chicago and berlin.

Technical experience: Motion Graphics   OCN Lighting L2

Phase One - Working alongside V.I artist's to present a live visual performance   (June 09)
6 Months Erasmus Exchange - Karlstad, Sweden (Jan 08 - June 08)
Developing understanding of Intercultural Communication, International Marketing and Global Media Trends, New Media and New Technology
Next Clothing - 1 week work experience shadowing executive advertiser and buyer (May 04)

References

John Parker-Rees FHEA
Senior Lecturer UCF
+44 (0)1326 370403
john.parker-rees@falmouth.ac.uk

Russel Clarke
Course leader UCF
+44 (0)1326 370403
russel.clarke@falmouth.ac.uk

SUPERPH🎧NO🎧

ANIMATION / ILLUSTRATION

Tamsin Baker
Animator : Illustrator

W: www.Tamsinbaker.com
e: taz@Tamsinbaker.com
T: 079 99 136 275
A: The Walnuts, Ashbury
SWINDON. sn6 8Ln.

PROFILE

I am a productive and highly motivated individual with a wide range of skills that incorporate both still and moving image as well as traditional and computer based work. I love the quirky and the unusual and try to bring energy and a fresh perspective to everything I do.

WORK & EXPERIENCE

Feb 2009 : Logo and designs completed for the Yellow Canary film production company
Nov 2008 : Animated credit sequence completed for short film 'The Bachelor Tree' (directed by Mark Turnock)
Jan 2008 : Full website commissioned by Bozley's Mobile Disco (www.bozleysmobiledisco.co.uk)
Jan 2008 : Animated credit sequence completed for short film 'Bubbles is a Stupid name' (directed by Jem Garrard)
Oct 2007 : 16 Illustrations commissioned by MySongCast.com
June – July 2007 : Employed as a Classroom assistant at Ashbury Preschool, working in busy environment with up to 18 children.
March & June 2007 : 25 Illustrations/Photoshop brushes commissioned by Frese Photography

EDUCATION

2006 – 2009 : UCA at Farnham
BA (Hons) Animation (Pending)
2004 – 2006 : New College, Swindon
Art and Design AVCE (AA), ICT A-level (B), English Language AS (B)
1999 – 2004 : Faringdon Community College
12 GCSEs (4 A*s, 6 As, 2 Bs)

Skills & Interests

I have expert knowledge of **Adobe Photoshop** and **Microsoft Office** and am proficient in the use of **After Effects** and **Flash** on both Mac and PC. In my own time I have also achieved a **mentoring** accreditation and learnt to **touch type**. I also regularly design and produce posters, CD covers and promotional material for numerous bands, small businesses and individuals. The rest of my time is spent writing, drawing, maintaining my e-commerce websites and decorating t-shirts and cakes for commission. In addition I have a clean driving licence and my own car. When not creatively engaged I like to skate and unicycle.

REFERENCES

Available on request

(Showreel and Gallery available at www.tamsinbaker.com)

FILM

Mike Linforth | Camera Department

'Hero' – Bombay, India, Autumn 2007

Personal Statement

I am a keen camera operator with a professional working ethos. I show commitment to learning the skills of cinematography, as well as dedication to the projects I have worked on. I pride myself on working on set under pressured situations. University has taught me how to utilise my technical knowledge and apply it to the creative aspects of my work. In 2008 I was the winner of the Dougie Slocombe Cinematography Scholarship awarded by Billy Williams.

Key Skills

Good Knowledge and experience shooting on many formats including:
- HDV +HD
- Super 8mm + Super16mm
- 35mm lens adapters (Redrock M2, Letus35)
- Comfortable loading Arriflex SR3,
- Experience in loading Arriflex 435, 535.
- Competent editor
- Knowledge of Avid media composer + Final Cut Pro
- Knowledge of sound equipment including Fostex FR2 and SQN mixers
- Experience in Producing and Assistant Directing

Qualifications

September 2005 – June 2008
University College for the Creative Arts, Farnham, Surrey
BA (Hons) Film Production – First Class

September 2002 – June 2004
Stratford-upon-Avon College, Stratford, Warwickshire
BTEC National Diploma Media Studies
Distinction, Distinction, Merit

September 1997 – June 2002
Southam Technology College, Southam, Warwickshire
9 GCSE's

Achievements

- Winner of Dougie Slocombe Cinematography 2007/2008 award
- Graduation film (Hero) Screen at Eat Our Shorts at BFI Southbank
- Graduation film selected for short film DVD
- Films screened at BFI film festivals – 'Eat Our Shorts' and 'BKSTS'

Contact details:
16 Bridge Square, Farnham, Surrey GU97QR
Telephone: 07870 819 183
Email: mike_linforth@hotmail.co.uk

'Hero' – Bombay, India, Autumn 2007

Professional Experience (selected credits)

From 2004 – 2005 I moved to Dubai to work for a film production company. I quickly found that
I was suited within the camera department, and began operating video playback on commercials.
This experience developed my passion for cameras, and my eye for creating images. Before I left,
I had the opportunity to work as a clapper loader on several shoots.

Date	Production Company	Client	Director	Job title
May 2008	KentLyons	Booktrust	N/A	Cinematographer
May 2005	Le Pac/Filmworks	Opel 'Zafira'	Frank Vroegop	VT Operator
Apr 2005	Filmworks	DSS	Franco Marinelli	VT Operator
Apr 2005	Filmworks	NCB	Derek Coutts	VT Operator
Apr 2005	Filmworks	NCB	Derrech Coutts	VT Operator
Mar 2005	Filmworks	Dubai Holding	Marc Chalhoub	VT Operator
Mar 2005	Filmworks	Finalcut Film Production	Amr Arafa	VT Operator
Mar 2005	Filmworks	Galaxy	Olavi Hakkinnen	VT Operator
Jan 2005	Boomtown Productions	Pepsi	Hady	VT Operator
Jan 2005	Filmworks	AFG	Franco Marinelli	VT Operator
Dec 2004	Valkieser Middle East	Sony Handy Cam	Hany Tamba	VT Operator
Dec 2004	Hot Dog Films/Filmworks	My Travel Channel	Nicholas Barker	VT Operator

Filmography (selected credits)

Date	Production	Role	Format	Running time
Apr 2008	Glass Half Empty	Cinematographer	S8mm	6 min
Mar 2008	Fragments	Cinematographer	S16mm	10 min
Feb 2008	Our Very Own England	Cinematographer	HDV	8 min
Dec 2007	Kodak: The Good	Cinematographer	S16mm	30 sec
Nov 2007	But Only Hope	Focus Puller	S16mm	10 min
Oct 2007	Hero	Cinematographer	Mini DV	14 min
Sep 2007	The Wise	Cinematographer	HDV	30 sec
Apr 2007	Within The Shadows	Cinematographer	S16mm	7 min
Feb 2007	UnChained	Cinematographer/Director	Mini DV	3 min

Contact details:
16 Bridge Square, Farnham, Surrey GU97QR
Telephone: 07870 819 183
Email: mike_linforth@hotmail.co.uk

FINE ART

Artist Statement
Christine Lobb

My research explores the tensions that arise from close examination of an object's function, specifically, the paradoxical ideas of fragility and protection.

Working in the mediums of sculpture, drawing and digital print, I am drawn to objects like shells and bubble wrap which we know are responsible for incubating life or preserving nostalgia, yet perversely, they too require careful handling. I am fascinated by the contradictions created when we consider the relationship between these objects' functions and their fragile materials and this makes me want to use their language to create new scenarios.

I am intrigued by the battle between 'effect' and 'honesty' within artworks. There is a tension between a desire for the work to remain raw and sincere and editing work so that that truth is disguised. The exhibition in the image below became a forum for the exploration of these issues. Using bubble wrap as a common material, I made a series of sculptures which I consider to be independent systems for analysing illusion and sincerity. In one set of sculptures, clear resin and fibre glass matting have been used to stiffen the bubble wrap into one static position. In another I have made stop-motion animations, another set are suspended in air using helium balloons and the final set use nothing but the bubble wrap itself. Each set of sculptures appears further down the scale of illusion than the previous one. Eventually, the method is completely honest. The exhibition itself may be described as a forum for comparing these four methods of manipulation. Ultimately, at this stage in my research, the viewer could make up their own mind.

Short Biography

Christine Lobb (b. 1980) holds a Bachelor of Fine Art from the Ruskin School of Drawing & Fine Art, Oxford University; and a Master of Arts, Fine Art from the University for the Creative Arts, Canterbury. She has received various awards including the Stour Valley Arts Student Bursary Award (2006) and has lectured at University for the Creative Arts, Canterbury and Ashford School of Art & Design. Exhibitions include *Seedy Rushes* (group show), *Botanic Gardens*, Oxford; *Size Matters* (solo show), Cyprus College of Art, Lempa, Cyprus and *Conversations*, (group show), UCA Canterbury.

Forum for the discussion of gravity, 2006. Helium, balloons, invisible thread, lead, fibre glass, bubblewrap. Dimensions variable.

christinelobb@gmail.com
07814 266964

Christine Lobb
Studio D, Meltdowns Studios
St Lawrence Industrial Estate
Manston Road, Ramsgate
Kent CT11 0QZ

Education

Sept 05 - Sept 06	Master of Fine Art *University for the Creative Arts, Canterbury*	The project revolved around sculpture's relationship with gravity and the plinth.
Oct 03 - June 04	Post Graduate Diploma in Fine Art *Cyprus College of Art, Lemba, Cyprus*	Intensive study into sculpture's relationship with fragility within the context of natural objects found in Cyprus.
Oct 00 - June 03	Bachelor of Fine Art (2:1) *Ruskin School of Drawing & Fine Art, Oxford University*	Sculpture: examining the role of the discarded object in relation to the art market; Art history: 1900 - 2003, Dissertation: the commodification of the art object.

Selected Achievements & Exhibitions

Jan 2009	First @ 108 Public Art Award *Royal British Society of Sculptors, London and Canary Wharf Group plc*	1 of 5 artists short listed and commissioned to create maquette and proposal for £10,000 commission. Proposals exhibited in group show at RBS, Chelsea.
Aug 2008 - Mar 2009	Artist in Residence & Exhibition *Through the Looking Glass, Maidstone Borough Council*	Awarded studio space for 3 months to research and realise a new body of work which was exhibited in the solo show *Wasp in a Wig*.
June 2006	Public Art Commission for Ashford *Stour Valley Arts / Ashford Council*	Commission to create a piece of work for the Ashford Memorial Gardens for Architecture Week.
May 2004	Artist in Residence *Art & Wild Nature Foundation, Episkopi, Cyprus*	Short drawing residency experimenting with unconventional drawing methods. Drawings selected for the *Art & Wild Nature Foundation's* collection.

Lecturing Experience

2004 - 2007	BA top-up, HND, BTEC Foundation, National Diploma *Ashford School of Art & Design*	Responsibilities: Planning and delivery of syllabus as part of teaching team; preparing and marking assessments and projects; contribution to curriculum development; liaising with Learning Support Assistants
	Part-time BA *University for the Creative Arts Canterbury*	to work with students with special needs; planning and delivering Key Skills lessons; classroom management; UCAS advice; interviewing, participation in open days
	BTEC Foundation, National Diploma *Isle of Man College of Further Education*	and induction sessions; practical demonstrations of techniques and processes.

Professional Development / Courses

May 2007	Sculpting a Living Seminars	Royal British Society of Sculptors
July - Oct 07	Entrepreneurship Training for Creatives	University for the Creative Arts, Canterbury
Sept 04 - June 05	City & Guilds Cert in Teaching 16+ Learners	Isle of Man College of Further Education

References

Available upon request

FASHION

Caroline Giselle Taylor

88 Green Acres, Gloucester Road, Purley, Surrey, AB1 2CD
Home: 01231231234   *Mobile*: 012345123123   *Email*: caroline.giselle.taylor@gmail.com

Profile

Hard-working, adaptable second year student of BA(Hons) Fashion Design. Confident with software such as Adobe Illustrator CS3, hand-rendered technical drawings and experience with industrial sewing machines, pattern cutting and design. Interested in all areas of the art world, with a love of travel and philosophy. Looking for a 6-week placement within a dynamic fashion studio; all tasks will be approached with enthusiasm and willingness to learn.

Previous Employment & Work Experience

Jul - Sept 2009, Apr - May 2009	Design/General Assistant at Neurotica. Designing swing tags and labels, and toiling garments for Neurotica for Topshop collection. Producing CAD spec drawings for mainline and Topshop range. Creating Press Gift Packs for AW09 Collection Launch.
Mar-Apr 2009	Design Assistant at Dorothy Perkins, Arcadia. Updating colour palettes and trendboards, design ideas and research for various design departments, 5 garments were sampled.
Aug – Sept 2008	Design/General Assistant at Neurotica, included designing invitations for the On|Off London Fashion Week show and helping backstage, assisting pattern makers, cutting sample garments, assisting at photoshoots, visiting the factory and print studios with an introduction to placement and repetitive screen printing.
July 2005	Work experience with Eyefix Silks International and Arabella B Clothing, London.
July 2004	Work experience at French Connection and Farhi as assistant to head designer of Women's Accessories. Work experience with Eyefix Silks International.

Education

2006 – present	University for the Creative Arts, Epsom. BA Hons Fashion Design.
2004 – 2006	Reigate Sixth Form College
1992 – 2004	Croham Hurst Independent School for Girls

Achievements

BTEC	Diploma in Foundation Art and Design (Merit)
A Levels	Philosophy (A), Psychology (B), Spanish (B), Fine Art (C)
GCSEs	10 GCSES, 1 A*, 5 As, 4 Bs
Other	Jubilee Scholarship at Croham Hurst Independent School for Girls Royal Insitute of Mathematics Masterclasses

References

Victoria McGrane
Fashion Designer/Company Owner
Neurotica
Unit 302
27B Belfast Road
London, N16 6UN
Tel: 07950534914

Written reference available upon request.

FASHION

123 Bright Star Walk
The Big City
Sunny Blighty

Phone: +44 (0) 71 23456789
E-mail: wincy@wincyyau.com
Web: www.wincyyau.com

Wincy Yau

Winner of Textiles Award Graduate Fashion Week 2006

1st Class Honours!
London College of Fashion
BA Fashion Design Technology:
Surface Textiles for Fashion

Central St Martins College of Art and Design
BTEC: Diploma Foundation Studies in Art & Design
PDU: Pattern Construction (Distinction)
Key Skills: Level 3 (Communications)

Tendring Technology College
11 GCSEs: grade A*-C

An award-winning, top banana of a graduate with a fantastic sense of colour! Extensive experience with high-end brands has confirmed strength in precision jobs and love of CAD. Enjoys being creative and 'hands-on' but is also very comfortable in front of a computer due to a 'geek-streak in personality. A very talented and versatile candidate.

Noted as one of Vogue.com's 'Hot Fifteen' graduates making a noise in the fashion world very soon.

Screen, sublimation and digital **Printing**
Machine, hand, and CAD/CAM **Embroidery**
Machine **KNITTING**
Hand and CAD **ILLUSTRATION**
Garment Production
Flat **Pattern Construction** for wovens and jerseys

Computer Skills:
- Apple OSX
- Windows XP
- Adobe Creative Suite
- Microsoft Office
- Microsoft Publisher
- Micrografix Designer

Professional Experience

BURBERRY
04/05/05-19/08/05
Womenswear CAD Team (contract)

- Produced pages for buyer's catalogues.
- Technical illustration.
- CAD alteration of print and weave designs.
- Liaising with manufacturing staff by phone and email.
- Managing textiles for buyers catalogues.
- Assisted in producing and amending line sheets.
- Conducting trend research.
- Making up trend and swatch packs to present to designers.

Jasmine Di Milo
15/03/05-29/04/05
Studio Assistant (placement)

- Sample cutting for delicate fabrics.
- Organising fabric and trimmings stock.
- Liaising with international textile agents on phone and email.
- Administration.

MICHIKO KOSHINO
26/01/05-15/02/05
Studio Assistant/Dresser (placement)

- Hand finishing textiles.
- Textile art.
- Dresser for A/W 05 catwalk show for mainline collection.

JONATHAN SAUNDERS
07/2004-09/2004
Studio Assistant (placement)

- Screen-printing.
- Technical drawing.
- Pattern alteration.
- Sample cutting.
- Produced hand drawn prints for production.
- Running general errands for S/S 05 catwalk show.

I ♥ TO MOSH

- Nationality: British
- Date of Birth: 03/09/1983
- Driving Licence: Full, clean
- Languages: English, Hakka (Chinese), Cantonese listener, basic French

Photos, illustrations and CV design ©Win-Sei Yau
wincyyau.com

TEXTILES

Artist and Designer
ELIZABETH HAMMOND

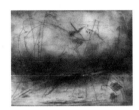 

www.elizabeth-hammond.com
elizabethhammondx@hotmail.co.uk

- An enthusiastic dedicated graduate committed to creative employment
- A creative individual with an attentive eye for detail
- An effective communicator who is confident and quick to learn

CREATIVE SKILLS

Drawing, Bookbinding, Printmaking including screen, mono, digital, etching and lino printing, Weaving, Felting, Embroidery (both hand and machine), Knitting, Weaving, Dyeing, Colour Theory and Generating Concept Ideas
Adobe Photoshop, In Design, Microsoft Word, CMS Intranet 200 and MS Power Point
Essential knowledge of Exposure Unit, Digital Printer, Steamer and Baker use

EDUCATION

Feb – Nov 2008   **Curtin University of Technology**
                        MA Visual Art

Sept 2003 – June 2006   **University College Falmouth**
                        BA (Hons) Textile Design

                        Student Representative for the course May 2006
                        Invigilated for the course at New Designers Exhibition 2005
                        Extensive involvement in the course which covered the development of design skills whilst also encouraging professional practice
                        In the degree chose to specialize in print, focusing on combining skills in art and design through traditional techniques in hand with contemporary practises

Sept 2002 – June 2003   **Winchester School of Art**
                        Foundation Diploma in Art and Design (Merit awarded)

Sept 2000 – June 2002   **Barton Peveril College, Eastleigh**
                        A Levels in Textiles (A), Fine Art (B) and English Literature (C)
                        AS Levels in Photography (C) and Drama and Theatre Studies (D)

CREATIVE EMPLOYMENT HISTORY

Aug 2009 – Current	**Sessional Academic Lecturer for Experimental Drawing and Textiles, Online Universities of Australia** Provide support and feedback on students' progress in the units Assess students' submissions in a timely and organised fashion
May 2009 - Current	**Tutor for Absolute Beginners Drawing, Fremantle Arts Centre** Write lesson plans and am conducting course to teach adults how to draw, give demonstrations, provide handouts and supply individual instruction
Sept 2008 – Sept 2009	**Tutor for Short Course Drawing Classes, Bentley** Wrote lesson plan and conducted course to teach all ages how to draw Gave demonstrations, provided handouts and supplied individual instruction
June 2008 – May 2009	**Graphic Artist for Little Design Horse, North Perth** Produced drawings for use in designs for the studio's portfolio
April 2009	**Tutor for Short Course Screen-printing Classes, Bentley** Wrote lesson plan and conducted a 6-week course to teach the process of screen-printing, gave demonstrations, provided handouts and supplied individual instruction
March 2006	**Clay Workshop Leader in the Design Centre for Widening Participation** Led a workshop instructing a class of 30 from a local school in the art of clay modelling Initiated skills and generated ideas to a group of children ages 9-10
Nov 2004 – June 2006	**Student Ambassador for University College Falmouth** Represented the University at UCAS fairs in London and Manchester Conducted tours of the University's Tremough Campus during Open Days Greeted Queen Elizabeth I and Duke of Edinburgh on their visit to Tremough Campus
Oct 2005	**Costume Designer for Falmouth Oyster Festival** Designed and produced the costume for the leading stilt artist "The Oyster Man"
July 2005	**Mentor for Creative Steps Summer School Falmouth** Responsible for the well fare of 25 young adults Motivated and provided technical assistance during a printmaking
May – June 2005	**Art Workshop Leader for Colour Explosion at The Eden Project in Cornwall** Worked closely with members of the general public to inspire them to enjoy the creative process of painting with no constrictions

PROFESSIONAL AFFILIATIONS   **Member of ArtSource, Artshub and Imprint**

REFEREES AVAILABLE ON REQUEST

TEXTILES

General Work Experience

Pizza Express - Kitchen Staff
February – June 2008, Falmouth

Troubadour Deli - Waitress
July 2007- December 2007, Earls Court, London

Nathan Associates - Office temp
March - April 2007, London

Huntress - Office temp
September 2007, Hammersmith, London

Mc Ewen & Parkinson - General assistant to solicitor
April & July 2004, London

Anne Fennell - Editors Assistant
June – July 2003, London

Education

1st Class BA Hons Textile Design
University College Falmouth 2006 - 2009

ABC Diploma in Foundatiom Art & Design (Distinction)
University College Falmouth 2004 - 2005

A-Level: Art (A), History (A), French (C)
10 GCSEs (A* - A)
St James Independent School For Girls 1990 - 2004

Exhibitions

Art in Action
July 2008, Arts & Crafts Festival, Oxford

Grape Lady Falls
June 2007, self curated group exhibition, Falmouth.

Farm W5
August 2004, self curated group exhibition, Ealing, London.

References
Available on request

Anna Glover

Work Experience

Liberty Art Fabrics - Work Placement in design studio.
August 2009

Circle Line - Work Placement in design studio.
July 2009

Eley Kishimoto - Work placement, Spring/Summer 09 Collection.
July – September 2008, London

Art in Action - Demonstrator and workshop assistant.
July 2008, Oxford

St James Independent School for Senior Girls - Assistant art teacher.
February -July 2006, Kensington Olympia, London

Decadent Dorothy - Handmade coats and skirts for S/S collection.
January – March 2006, Spitalfields, London

Noa Noa - Sales assistant, merchandising, shop and window displays.

Henry & Daughter - Studio and shop assistant in Made to measure
wedding dress boutique.
March – May 2003, Camden, London

Attributes
Good time management
Effective problem solver
Excellent eye for detail
Good eye for layout and composition
Strong illustrative drawing style
Fast learner
Confident communication skills
Approachable personality
Responsible

Skills
- High level of manual textile printing
- Proficient CAD and digital print skills
- Confident in Photoshop & Microsoft Office
- Intermediate Scatterware and digital jacquard
- Basic Pattern cutting & garment construction
- Good machine and hand sewing skills

Profile

As a textile designer I am interested in creating high quality, individual fabrics that tell stories. My specialist area is manual screen printing; I use this to create multi-layered illustrative textiles. In addition to this I work with both digital print and jacquard. This diverse combination of media allows fine drawing, bold pattern work and collaged imagery to be used simultaneously.

As an individual I am confident and hardworking. I am both organised and work well to deadlines or under pressure. Although generally quite independent, I also work well alongside other people and have excellent communication skills.

Anna Glover
Textile Designer
23 Kerrison Road, London, W5 5NW
anna@uglovers.net
+44(0)7977 515 102

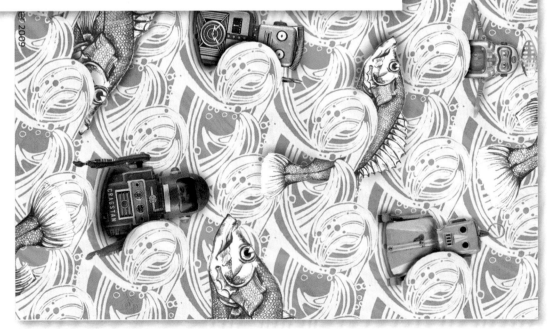

ANNA GLOVER, UNIVERSITY COLLEGE FALMOUTH

ENVIRONMENT

Education

Oct 05 - Jun 08   University College Falmouth, Cornwall
BA Hons Garden Design: Arts and Environment

Successful completion of the course has allowed me to develop confident computer, drawing and visualisation skills as well as sound horticultural knowledge, aided by part-time lectures at Duchy college, Rosewarne.
Having written a dissertation on the development of outdoor school environments, I developed a keen interest in the subject, which required me to undertake extensive research.

During the final year I was elected student representative for the third year garden design course. This role relied on good communication and organisational skills. It also introduced me to the formalarities of commitee meetings.

Sep 02 - Jul 04   Rugby High Grammar School
Rugby, Warwickshire
- A-level Art, A; Design and Technology, A; German, A

Sep 97 - Jul 02   Daventry William Parker School
Daventry, Northamptonshire
- 11 GCSEs grades A* - B including English, B; Maths, A; Science, B.

Exhibitions

Feb 07   Penryn Community Project, Cornwall
Exhibited design proposals for the redevelopment of Penryn playing field in Penryn town hall

Dec 07   Cornwall Design Week
An annual event for a variety of design disciplines.
Exhibited design proposals for a private family garden near Falmouth, Cornwall.

Work Experience

Apr 08 - Jun 08   Garden desi
in Buckingh

Apr 07 - Jul 07   Waitress, The

May 06 - Oct 07   Conference
Hotel, Fawsle

Sep 04 - Oct 04   Sorter/Packe
packaging m
Melbourne,

Aug 04   Chaperone, F

Aug 02 - Aug 06   Banqueting/
porter, Paran
Northampto

Awards

Sep 07   Society of Garden Designers, Student Garden Designer of theYear - 1st prize.
Submitted a second year design project for a private garden, including planting plans, client brief and masterplan.

Certificates

Jun 06   Royal Horticultural Society Level 2 Certificate in Horticulture
- Planning principles and production
- Ornamental principles and maintenance

Jun 07   Royal Yachting Association Level 1 and 2 Sailing

Aug 04   Sustainable Design Award, Design and Technology

Dec 00   Bronze Duke of Edinburgh Award

Computing

- European Computer Driving License - including word processing, spreadsheets, powerpoint presentations, information and communication
- Completed courses in Adobe Photoshop, Indesign and Illustrator as well as Dreamweaver
- Proficient in Autocad and Sketchup.

Language

- Fluent in German - both writing and speaking

nd ran 'creative thinking' workshops with hool children across Cornwall along side artnerships. This included digital animation s creative multi media exercises.

der   Pam Halsey - conference and banqueting manager
Paramount Daventry Hotel
Sedgemoor Way
Daventry
Northants NN11 5SG

01327 307000

Hallenga and Bugg
Landscape Design

Maren Hallenga
07707510588

maren@hblandscapedesign.com

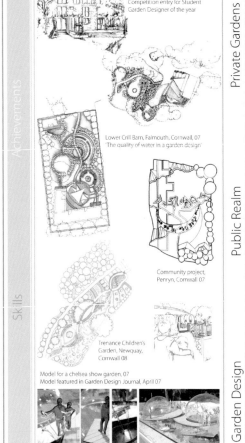

Butlers Quarry, Falmouth, Cornwall, 07
Competition entry for Student Garden Designer of the year

Lower Crill Barn, Falmouth, Cornwall, 07
'The quality of water in a garden design'

Community project, Penryn, Cornwall 07

Trenance Children's Garden, Newquay, Cornwall 08

Model for a chelsea show garden, 07
Model featured in Garden Design Journal, April 07

Private Gardens

Achievements

Public Realm

Garden Design

PHOTOGRAPHY

Sveinung Skaalnes is a creative.

INFORMATION

UK +44 (0) 7891 710 592
NO +47 911 98 983
SWE +46 (0) 7860 905 611
info@skaalnes.com
www.skaalnes.com

EDUCATION

**HYPER ISLAND
STOCKHOLM, SWEDEN**
hyperisland.com
INTERACTIVE ART DIRECTOR
August 2009 – Present

**UNIVERSITY COLLEGE FOR THE
CREATIVE ARTS – FARNHAM, UK**
ucreative.ac.uk
BA HONS PHOTOGRAPHY, 2.1
2004 – 2007

**ROBERT MEYER COLLEGE OF ART
OSLO, NORWAY**
BA PHOTOGRAPHY & DIGITAL MEDIA
2003 – 2004

ADDITIONAL SKILLS & INFO

Literate and confident on both Mac and PC,
with advanced experience in *Adobe Photoshop,
InDesign and Dreamweaver CS4, Lightroom 2* and
Capture One.

+ Norwegian (mother tongue)
+ English (fluent)
+ Born in Norway, 13.07.1984
+ Full Clean UK / EU Drivers Licence
+ First Aid training

EXHIBITIONS & PUBLICATIONS

BLUSS
August 2008
Group exhibition, with *'Pictures of Odd'*, Ven-
terommet Gallery – Mandal, Norway

TECHNIQUE
June 2008
Group exhibition, with *'Hello Darkness My Old
Friend'*, J. Hockey Gallery – UK

CLOSED CHAPTER
December 2007
Solo exhibition, Kulturfabrikken Gallery –
Mandal, Norway

CREATIVE REVIEW BLOG
June 2007
Featured in *'Best Degree Show Work 2007'* with
'Pictures of Odd' – London, UK

DOT DOT DOT
June 2007
Group exhibition, with *'Pictures of Odd'*, Tru-
man Brewery – London, UK

FREELANCE ROLES

**UNIVERSITY FOR THE CREATIVE
ARTS, FARNHAM**
ucreative.ac.uk
SESSIONAL LECTURER
August 2008 – Present
I lecture on all three years of the BA Hons Pho-
tography. As unit leader I schedule and run tu-
torials and creative technical workshops in the
studios. I run creative idea based workshops on
BA Hons Graphic Communication.

PHOTOGRAPHER JASON EVANS
jasonevans.info
PRODUCER
June 2006 – May 2009
Production of jobs and commissions; managing projects from start to finish, including negotiation and budgeting; ranging within music,
editorial, fashion and advertising.

JASMINE STUDIOS
jasminestudios.com
STUDIO ASSISTANT
March 2006 – August 2009
Dealing with high-profile personalities, low-
profile briefs, extreme demand clients, solving
unsolvable problems & being one step ahead.

SELECTED PROJECTS

I HATE MY FEET
October 2009 / ihatemyfeet.com
Commisioned interviews and editorial fashion
photography, online magazine – London, UK

CYCLE CHIC
June 2009 / warehouse.co.uk
Editorial photography for Warehouse Fashion
Ltd – London, UK

BEHIND SS09
September 2008 / richardnicoll.com
Editorial photography for womanswear
designer Richard Nicoll – London, UK

VATLE SS09
July 2008 / vatledesigns.com
Lookbook and Editorial photography for womenswear designer Kjersti Vatle, Oslo Fashion Week – Oslo, Norway

SIMIAN MOBILE DISCO
August 2007 / simianmobiledisco.com
Editorial photography for Guitar Center Mag-
azine (US) – London, UK

THREE WARDROBES AW08
September 2007 / sivstoldal.com
Lookbook for designer Siv Stoldal at London
Fashion Week – London, UK

PROSPECTUS
June 2007 / ureative.ac.uk
Creative Marketing brief, UCA – UK

All references are available on request.

PERMANENT ROLES

HARPER'S BAZAAR - UK
harpersbazaar.co.uk
ONLINE EDITORIAL ASSISTANT
May 2009 – August 2009
My role included writing and editing all news
and features covering the areas of Fashion and
Going Out on *harpersbazaar.co.uk*; researching
and writing weekly features and daily news;
building and maintaining all content in CMS.

**UNIVERSITY FOR THE CREATIVE
ARTS, FARNHAM**
ucreative.ac.uk
*TUTOR TECHNICIAN IN DIGITAL PHO-
TOGRAPHY*
July 2007 – August 2008
My main area of responsibility was the development and day-to-day management of the
digital post-production suites. This included
pre- and post-production of material for out-
put – both on site – and pre-press production
for offset printing at external facilities, producing print work to an excellent standard.

SELECTED CLIENTS

*SIESEIDO / HANATSUBAKI
STELLA McCARTNEY / ADIDAS
EMI RECORDS
PARTNER+PARTNER
RICHARD NICOLL
SIV STOLDAL
SIMIAN MOBILE DISCO
TWENTYSIX LETTERS LTD
I HATE MY FEET
WAREHOUSE
FANTASTIC MAN MAGAZINE
ID MAGAZINE
JASON EVANS
PATRICIA VON AH*

ARCHITECTURE

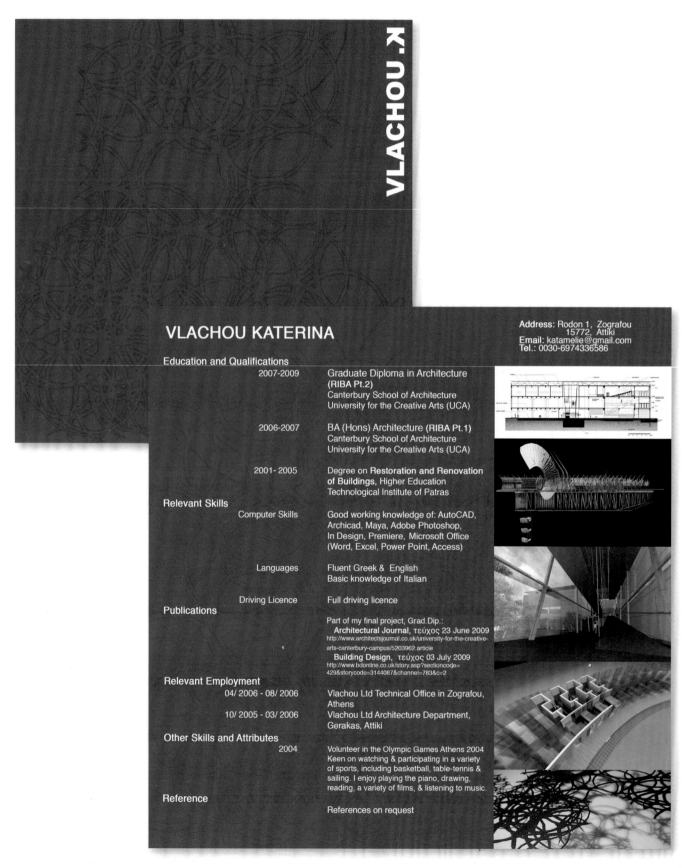

VLACHOU .K.

VLACHOU KATERINA

Address: Rodon 1, Zografou
15772, Attiki
Email: katamelie@gmail.com
Tel.: 0030-6974336586

Education and Qualifications

2007-2009	Graduate Diploma in Architecture (RIBA Pt.2) Canterbury School of Architecture University for the Creative Arts (UCA)
2006-2007	BA (Hons) Architecture (RIBA Pt.1) Canterbury School of Architecture University for the Creative Arts (UCA)
2001- 2005	Degree on **Restoration and Renovation of Buildings,** Higher Education Technological Institute of Patras

Relevant Skills

Computer Skills	Good working knowledge of: AutoCAD, Archicad, Maya, Adobe Photoshop, In Design, Premiere, Microsoft Office (Word, Excel, Power Point, Access)
Languages	Fluent Greek & English Basic knowledge of Italian
Driving Licence	Full driving licence

Publications

Part of my final project, Grad.Dip.:
Architectural Journal, τεύχος 23 June 2009
http://www.architectsjournal.co.uk/university-for-the-creative-arts-canterbury-campus/5203962.article
Building Design, τεύχος 03 July 2009
http://www.bdonline.co.uk/story.asp?sectioncode=429&storycode=3144087&channel=783&c=2

Relevant Employment

04/ 2006 - 08/ 2006	Vlachou Ltd Technical Office in Zografou, Athens
10/ 2005 - 03/ 2006	Vlachou Ltd Architecture Department, Gerakas, Attiki

Other Skills and Attributes

2004	Volunteer in the Olympic Games Athens 2004 Keen on watching & participating in a variety of sports, including basketball, table-tennis & sailing. I enjoy playing the piano, drawing, reading, a variety of films, & listening to music.

Reference

References on request

KATERINA VLACHOU, UNIVERSITY FOR THE CREATIVE ARTS

JEWELLERY

EDUCATION & QUALIFICATIONS
BA (Hons) Jewellery Design, First Class
Central Saint Martins College of Art and Design, UAL, 2004-2007
Foundation Studies Art and Design, Distinction
Camberwell College of Arts, UAL, 2003-2004
Pre-Foundation Art
Community Education Lewisham, 2003
BMus (Hons) 2:1 (Bassoon)
Guildhall School of Music and Drama, London, 1996-2000

COURSES
Photoshop - Level 2, University of the Arts London, 2009
Small Leather Accessories, London College of Fashion, 2009
Rhino - Intermediate, Holts Academy, London, 2008
Adobe Illustrator for Technical Drawing and Product Design,
Holts Academy, London, 2008
Rhino - Beginners, Holts Academy, London, 2008
'Getting Started' Goldsmiths' Hall, London, 2008
Flying Start Programme for Women Entrepreneurs, York, 2008

COMPETITIONS & AWARDS
Holts Academy, 3-D Design Award, Commendation, 2008
Creative Careers CV Design Competition, Joint Winner, 2007
New Designers The Goldsmiths' Company Jewellery Award, Winner, 2007
Links of London Group Project Competition, Winner, 2006
Swarovski Prize, Category Winner, 2005

EMPLOYMENT HISTORY
Assistant CAD/CAM Service Technician, H3-d, London, 2009 - Present
Library Assistant, London College of Fashion, UAL, 2007-2009
Library Resources Assistant, Central Saint Martins, UAL, 2005-2007
Administrator, Christian Aid, London, 2005
Administrator, Health & Safety Executive, London, 2001-2002

SELECTED EXHIBITIONS
Collections, Earls Court, London, 2008
Winter Design Collection, The Billcliffe Gallery, Glasgow, 2007
New Designers Selection, OXO Tower, London, 2007
Top Drawer Autumn, Olympia, London, 2007
New Designers, Business Design Centre, London, 2007

WORK EXPERIENCE
Links of London, 2008
Hannah Martin, 2006

SKILLS
Photoshop, Illustrator, InDesign,
Rhino, RhinoGold, Matrix 3D

SARAH VELAZCO

Flat 1, 58A Martins Road,
London, NW6 3CV
info@sarahvelazco.co.uk
www.sarahvelazco.co.uk
07714 720 235

SARAH VELAZCO, UNIVERSITY OF THE ARTS LONDON

SPATIAL DESIGN

Charlotte Burden
BA (Hons) Spatial Design

Charlotte Burden . . . . profi

Trinity Place
Hill Road
Plymouth
Devon
PL1 5TB

charlotte_b@hotmail.com
tel: 07754287543
D.O.B 18/10/85

I am a creative and enthusiastic designer, who enjoys both interior and exterior design. A reliable, conscientious and flexible team worker, I am well organised, confident and quick to learn.

My particular interest within Spatial design lies in the remodelling and creative reuse of old existing buildings and spaces. Much of my work is site responsive, and sensitive to the context and quality of the location. My aim is to further my knowledge and experience in this field and work as part of a team to produce innovative designs.

Images of my work:

Truro Cathedral

PRODUCT DESIGN

SparksDesign

Sarah Parks
3D Designer Maker

Email: parks_43286@hotmail.com
Website: www.sparksdesign.moonfruit.com

Profile

Sarah Parks

Current address	Home Address
13 Wellington Terrace	La Falaise
Falmouth	Havelet
Cornwall	St Peter port
TR11 3BN	Guernsey
	GY1 1BA

Tel: 01326 314418 (Falmouth)   Tel: 01481 724975 (Guernsey)   Mobile: 097

Email: parks_43286@hotmail.com
Website: www.sparksdesign.moonfruit.com

I am an excellent communicator and extremely organized, enabling me to meet tigh deadlines. I thrive on new challenges and am a team player. I am a dedicated des maker and I am interested in all areas of design, especially sustainable products a furniture. As an undergraduate I have access to many different resources and lectu visiting speakers.

Key strengths:	Research - Research into materials - User centred design
	Innovative
	Team player
	Multiskilled

Aspirations:	To gain a wide experience in product design
	To have the opportunity to research sustainable materials
	To learn from different designers through working alongside them
	To become a significant designer

Examples of my work

education and qualifications

niversity College Falmouth
ep 2004 - June 2007 BA(Hons) First Class Spatial Design.

y degree in Spatial Design combines creative skills and conceptual thinking with
chnical knowledge and practical model making techniques within a variety of
ojects.

ojects completed include:
The Foundry: new space, new community - a new heart for an historically
important site.
Evoking the Past - the creative reuse of St. Day old Trinity Church.
Truro Cathedral precinct area - a landscape scheme.
Live project - designing the exhibition stand fro New Designers, London '06.

ep 2003 - June 2004 Art Foundation Diploma / Grade Distinction.
nal project work was displayed in an exhibition in Falmouth Arts Centre.

ep 2001 - June 2003 Bruton School for Girls Sixth Form College.
levels in Art, Design and Technology and Biology.
ades A, A, B achieved respectively. Also awarded Cumberlige Art Scholarship
d the Sixth Form Design and Technology award for 2003.

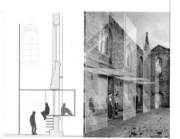

skills and experience

Design Skills:

Hand drawing and clear 2D graphic design skills, conceptual thinking, technical
drawing and detailing, photography and confidence in verbally and visually
communicating my ideas. I have good 3D model making capabilities and take
pride in producing high quality models. In 2006 I was chosen to present my
model of Truro Cathedral to the Queen on her visit to UCF.

I am also proficient in using software such as Photoshop, InDesign, Sketchup and
AutoCAD.

Experience:

Gilmore Hankey Kirke Architects, Plymouth (Sep 2007 - present)
Working as an architectural assistant completing planning application packages,
survey work, graphic presentation and feasibility studies, as well as managing
certain projects.

I particularly enjoy meeting clients and site work with contractors and have gained
valuable knowledge of professional practice.

Workhouse Architects studio, Tr
During my work placement m
of a particular building pr
drawings and images for
competition brief.

Katherine Fortescue Ltd.
Here I worked on interior la
for interior furnishings and s
office work such as orders an

References available on Req

Course Leader from University
andrew.harbert@falmouth.ac.uk

CHARLOTTE BURDEN, UNIVERSITY COLLEGE FALMOUTH

cation and Qualifications

cation

ersity College Falmouth   **2007 - Current**
I am currently studying a BA Hons Degree in 3D Design.
Sustainable design is the core theme of the degree. All aspects of this are covered
including theory, materials and design.
Subjects comprise, community and user centre design, inclusive design, sustainable
design and broad knowledge of materials.
During my degree I have worked with various companies, such as Move Virgo, who
specialise in UV resin and Cloud Nine. A woven structure developed to strengthen the
resin was incorporated in an Exhibition by Ben Cook, Artist in Residence, at the Eden
Project. I am currently working on a group project with Barncrest, designing a product
utilising their off-cuts.

gston University   **2006 - 2007**
Art & Design Foundation Degree, Merit.

Ladies' College Guernsey   **91999 - 2006**
A-Levels in Art & Design (A), Design Technology: Product Design (A), History (D)
AS-Level in Business Studies (C)
GNVQ Young Enterprise Credit
10 GCSE's (A* - B)
City & Guild Award - IT

er Qualifications

s a competition prize winner for Barncrest, March 2009, for my 'Stoolbench' design.
k part in the Young Enterprise Scheme and was the Operations Director gaining a credit in
optional GNVQ. It was a great experience learning from experts and working in a group
t up a profitable company.
e achieved the Gold Duke of Edinburgh Award, First Aid, Life Saving Bronze Award
Day Skipper, RYA Sailing Instructor, RYA Competent Crew, VHF Licence and a Full driving
ce.

Skills and Experience

Design Skills

Community & sustainable design
Extensive materials knowledge
Proficient materials research skills

Workshop Skills

CNC Router
Laser Cutter
Woodwork skills

IT Skills

Photoshop
Illustrator
InDesign
Autodesk 3D Studio Max
Solidworks
Moonfruit Site Maker

Experience

At university I am a Student Mentor and am a volunteer for the FXU Community Action Society.
I am also learning Italian at night classes.
I helped Cloud Nine at Grand Designs Live 2009, learning about eco-living and the methods
used to reach it.
Throughout my sixth form years I was a volunteer for the Guernsey Millennium Tapestry and
took part in life drawing night classes to enhance my drawing ability.
I attended a course; Sculpture from Scrap Metal using Blacksmithing Techniques at West Dean
College, April 2006.
From 2004 - 2009 I have had the following jobs: Banking Administrator, Scarborough CI;
Sales Assistant, B&Q; RYA Sailing Instructor, Guernsey Sailing Trust and Sales Assistant, Boots
the Chemist.

Referees available on Request

SARAH PARKS, UNIVERSITY COLLEGE FALMOUTH

ACADEMIC

LUCY GUNDRY

Mobile Number

1 The Street   University for the Creative Arts
City-upon-Thames   Faulkner Road
County   Farnham
Postcode   Surrey, GU9 7DS
Personal email   Work email

Profile

My main research interests lie in the field of textiles/fashion and relate to the contextual and contemporary issues around the body, identity and exhibition, situated in material, visual and consumer cultures.

Future plans are to continue my professional development in learning and teaching practice and research at FE and HE level, alongside personal research to PhD level. My future line of enquiry is looking at the role of the mannequin in the dichotomy between function and fantasy from the street to the gallery disseminated on www.otherbody.com.

Education

2007 - 2008   **MA Museums and Contemporary Curating (Distinction)**
University for the Creative Arts
'Curating the Corporeal: Mannequin, Model and Muse' (Dissertation)

1998 - 2001   **BA (Hon's) Textile Art** Winchester School of Art
'Materialisation of paper in Japan' (Dissertation)

1991 - 1994   **BA (Hon's) History of Design and the Visual Arts** Staffordshire University
'The Ikonoclastic sub-culture of Graffiti Art' (Dissertation)

Awards

2007- 8   Arts and Humanities Research Council (AHRC) - Full Postgraduate Award
2000   The Textile Society Bursary
1999 & 2000   Richmond Parish Lands - Student Bursary

Publications

2009   *Fusing Craft and Technology.* A-N Newsletter, May 2009, pp. 17.
2008   *Fabricated Skins.* Textile: The Journal of Cloth and Culture, 6(3), pp. 286–291.
2008   Ten Artists Profiles. In Monem, Nadine ed. *Contemporary Textiles: The Fabric of Fine Art,* pp. 74-75. London: Black Dog Publishing.
2006   *Notes taken by Lucy Gundry 'Outcomes Seminar 1: Ambiguous Spaces 2'.* http://www.contextandcollaboration.com/seminar1_notes.html
2003   Concealing and Revealing. *Embroidery Magazine,* 54, pp. 30.
2001   Japanese Kamiko. *TEXT For the Study of Textile Art, Design and History,* 29(2001-2), pp. 28-29.

Professional Development / Research

2009   C&G 7303 Preparing to Teach in the Life Long Learning Sector: Level 4
2009   Visual Research Methodologies research (HEA) - University for the Creative Arts
2006   Textile exhibition and audience research – University for the Creative Arts
2000   Set up exchange between Winchester School of Art and   Kawashima Textile School, Kyoto, Japan.

Teaching Experience

2003	Visiting Tutor - Richmond Adult and Community College
	BTEC Art & Design Foundation (Textile/Fashion)
2003	Workshop Leader - Thames Valley University
	Working in Costume for TV/Film (one day)

Employment

Learning and Teaching Project Researcher (0.4) - University for the Creative Arts
Feb 2009 – Nov 2009
- Contextual review of visual research methodologies.
- Conference paper case study research/writing and collaborative presentation with Q&A.
- Set up and conducting interviews/workshops with post graduate UCA students.

Part-time Tutor - Richmond Adult and Community College
Sept 2009 - Ongoing
- Textile/Fashion - Research/contextual and exhibition modules (NOCN/BTEC/vocational)

Editorial Assistant (0.1 Voluntary) - Textile: The Journal of Cloth and Culture
Feb 2009 – Ongoing
- Coordination of abstracts, papers, peer reviews and images with authors, editors and publishers.

Textile Futures Research Group Administrator 0.4 - University of the Arts London
May 2007 – May 2008
- Managing internal and external meetings/workshops/seminars with website/IT (video/audio) collaboration with partnership organisations (ICA/Furtherfield) and UAL academic staff/students.
- Sourcing/collating/disseminating information for partners/team members/website.
- Writing material, producing, maintaining, archiving website pages and images.

Skills & Knowledge

Academic	Contemporary & contextual knowledge of textile/fashion/applied arts & visual arts in relation to exhibition/visual/material and consumer cultures.
Research	Sourcing, selecting, analyzing and writing up research material.
Administrative	ICT, Microsoft Office, interpersonal, organisational and problem solving.
Practical	Knowledge of textile / fashion processes, practices and applications.

Conferences

Sept 2009	1st International Visual Research Methods Conference – collaborative presentation Q&A on visual research methods – University of Leeds.
Dec 2005	Context and Collaboration 'Ambiguous Spaces 2' Seminar – presentation of 'Breakout Group Report' - AHRC funded and held at UCA, Farnham.

Professional Membership

Institute for Learning – Associate

References

Hannah Gail (Employer)
Dean of Learning & Teaching
University for the Creative Arts
Faulkner Road, Farnham,
Surrey. GU9 7DS

Prof. Linda May (MA Tutor)
University for the Creative Arts
Ashley Road
Epsom,
Surrey, KT18 9BY

MAKING CONTACT

Although it may be the last thing you write, the cover letter or email will probably be the first thing read by the recipient and, as such, is likely to make an initial and lasting impression. Its purpose is to introduce you and your CV, offer a clear explanation of why you are writing and link your interests, skills and experience to the company or department. As with all communication, it is vital that you demonstrate you are able to conduct matters in a competent and businesslike manner.

Take the trouble to find out about the person to whom you are writing. What is their name and position? What can you find out about their work, their clients or their professional interests? Indicate your interest in them, and, if possible, make links to your own work and personal qualities. Company websites and professional journals frequently provide a wealth of information to help you make these connections.

Be explicit about what you are seeking, such as a work placement, a job or information. Give dates of your availability and outline your objectives. It is important to be realistic about what you might achieve. For instance, as a work placement student, it is unlikely that you will be let loose on a multi-million pound project, but just observing, supporting and networking are hugely valuable at this stage of your career.

Outline how your skills, experience and interests match the requirements of the company. Try not to fall into the trap of concentrating solely on yourself, but make it clear how you could benefit the company. You need to convince the reader that you have done some research, understand the business and the role, and that you would be a useful asset to them. Although it is very important to be positive about yourself, there is a fine line between communicating your strengths and sounding overconfident or even arrogant.

The tone can also help to create a lasting impression. Try to be yourself, whilst being professional. Basic research should provide some vital clues as to the type of language and approach that would be most appropriate, i.e. a very formal company would probably prefer a more formal approach, whilst another organisation may appreciate a touch of humour or innovation.

Although you should avoid simply repeating information contained in your CV, the covering correspondence is an opportunity to elaborate on key points and contextualise information so its relevance to the position is made clear.

This may be an appropriate place to disclose a disability, account for a gap in your employment or even to offer an explanation of facts that are contained in, or lacking from, your CV. However, this is a judgement call and a lot will depend on the purpose of your CV and how comfortable you feel about declaring such information at this stage.

EXPERT OPINION

Gary Lin

66 A short cover letter makes all the difference. Many candidates don't even have a cover letter, which makes their effort seem insincere. Once you have sent a CV, always follow it up until you know that the person you've sent it to has read it."
Gary Lin – Head Designer, **still waters run deep**

ANNA GLOVER
UNIVERSITY COLLEGE FALMOUTH

MAKING CONTACT
(CONT.)

The letter or email should be quite short. No more than one page at the most. If you feel it necessary to provide substantially more information in order to enhance your application, then it is advisable to attach an 'Additional Information' sheet to the application form. Be aware that word counts and limited space are often used to test an applicant's ability to be succinct.

Finally, be prepared to follow up the contact if you do not receive a reply within a reasonable time. With the best will in the world, it is easy for a busy manager to overlook, or put to one side, a speculative CV. Most employers do not take offence to a short and polite follow-up call in response to an unanswered communication. It only goes to emphasise just how much you want to visit or join the organisation.

Email or letter?
The choice of whether you communicate by letter or email may be partly a matter of personal preference but should also take into account any protocol or preference by the company. A printed letter is also slightly more formal and provides greater control over the final presentation of your documents.

Email etiquette
Even though you may be communicating by email, it is still important to maintain a certain level of formality, especially when making initial contact. Start your email 'Dear ....' (not Hi), never use text abbreviations and above all, **never** 'cc' 20 other companies. The same rules apply to writing a personalised, individual communication, whether sending a letter or email.

CHECKLIST

- ✔ Thoroughly research the organisation and the individual before writing.

- ✔ Address correspondence to a named person.

- ✔ Tell the organisation why you want to work for them.

- ✔ Refer to specific skills and interests that link you to the organisation and/or the job.

- ✔ Make it clear why you are writing, i.e. applying for an advertised position, requesting a work placement.

- ✔ Ensure your correspondence complements and enhances your CV.

- ✔ Ensure your correspondence portrays you as keen, capable and professional.

- ✔ Ask one or two trusted supporters to read and check your application (preferably someone with experience of viewing CVs).

EXPERT OPINION

LizRoberts

❝ Don't go on about how the job will be great for your own personal development, rather than about what you can offer to the publication. Tailor your application to the job/organisation. Make sure you say why you would be good for that particular job. Explain why you are interested in the subject matter and spell out what skills and experience you have that are relevant. Often I get covering letters that just say in so many words, 'I want to apply for this job. I am really good'. Or I'm told how much someone loves motor sport, but not a thing about why early years education would be interesting. Get the balance right between giving enough details and not being too verbose. I want a journalist to be concise, but I want enough to be able to judge whether to interview them. Writing style should be clear and literate – don't try to prove how 'creative' you are."

Liz Roberts – Editor, ***Nursery World***

COVER LETTERS

JOB APPLICATION

21 Nonsuch Square
Fiction Street
London HE LLO

Tel: 07699 588 662
catherineljdouglas@hotmail.co.uk

Design Studios

07/02/2008

Dear Mr Watson

RE: Graphic Designer role

I'm interested in applying for the position above which was advertised through the Creative Careers website. I've had a range of work experience and freelancing at various types of agencies including packaging design, print design, branding, advertising and experience design. I have also held an admin position, giving a total of 18 months experience.

Graduating from Chelsea College of Arts, I received the 1st prize D&AD award for my entry promoting Parlophone's music artists in a festival environment in a really fun and engaging way (see samples).

I express myself openly and clearly with colleagues, verbally and in written communication. I enjoy working as part of a team and I am a busy-body, ensuring that I always use my self-initiative and work on the targets at hand, which means that I am motivated to work unsupervised and be resourceful in order to overcome barriers that may arise. I'm very organised and work proficiently in all MS Office applications, Adobe Photoshop, InDesign, Illustrator and Quark Xpress, with an average typing speed of 90 words per min. I consider that I would be a positive asset to your organisation as I am a reliable, honest and motivated person.

Currently I am designing the front-end of a social networking website that is due to launch this year and have recently worked on rebranding ethical clothes company 'Tam and Rob'.

Best regards,
Catherine Douglas

Please see my CV overleaf, please contact me if you'd like to discuss anything further.

CATHERINE DOUGLAS, UNIVERSITY OF THE ARTS LONDON

FREELANCE

Mike Linforth | Camera Department

'Hero' – Bombay, India, Autumn 2007

Aneta Weedon
Human Resources
Talkback THAMES
20–21 Newman Street
London W1T 1PG

16 July 2008

Dear Ms Aneta Weedon

I am applying for your advert for freelance rigger/driver at The Bill.

I am a hard working, dedicated and passionate person and believe my work is evidence of this. My professional experience and chosen specialist path through University has given me the skills detailed in your job advert along with the foundations to build upon to succeed in my career.

Upon completing a media course in 2004, I moved to Dubai to work for a production house as a runner. After a few weeks of training, I moved to work with the camera department as a VT operator. I began assisting the (then) current operator on commercials, and soon took over this position. Over the following months, I worked on productions for clients such as Snickers, Pepsi, Opel and Ford with budgets in excess of £1,000,000.

During these shoots I became competent operating on formats from VHS to Mini DV to Hard Drive on multi-camera set-ups. I worked well under the extreme pressures, always conducting myself with professionalism when addressing crew, the director and clients.

Since returning to England, I have completed a BA Honours in Film and Video Production at University College of the Creative Arts gaining a First Class degree. During these 3 years, I have dedicated everything to my work, which is evident in my showreel. At the beginning of 2008, I was awarded the Dougie Slocombe Scholarship for Cinematography, presented by Billy Williams. The course has equipped me to work on all aspects of production.

Please consider me for this position. I feel I can fulfil everything you require, and believe this will be a fantastic opportunity for the start of my career.

Thank you for your time.

Yours sincerely

Mike Linforth

Contact details:
16 Bridge Square, Farnham, Surrey GU97QR
Telephone: 07870 819 183
Email: mike_linforth@hotmail.co.uk

MIKE LINFORTH, UNIVERSITY FOR THE CREATIVE ARTS

EMAIL EXAMPLES

INTERNSHIP

FROM: Simona Bartini. simona.bartini@webmail.co.uk
TO: Janine Gregory, janine@edwardevans.webmail
SUBJECT: Internship

FOR THE ATTENTION OF:
Janine Gregory,
Curator
The Edward Evans Gallery

Dear Ms. Gregory,

Firstly, I would like to thank you for giving such an interesting and informative talk to the Fine Art students on the subject of working with galleries. During your presentation you mentioned that the Edward Evans Gallery offered seasonal internships during the summer and I am writing to enquire further about this opportunity.

I am a keen and frequent visitor to the Edward Evans Gallery and have found your contemporary collection to be both inspirational and thought provoking. I was so inspired by the work of John Harrison displayed in your gallery that for my dissertation I have made a comparison of his work and influences with that of other 20th century artist's living on the South Coast.

As you will see from the attached CV, I have developed strong administration skills through my part-time work at KKS & Partners. In addition, my Fine Art studies have required me to undertake meticulous research which I have logged for ease of reference. Last Summer I was a member of the organising committee for our interim course show which involved liaising with both the gallery manager and other students. Although I will, of course be bringing these skills to the gallery, the most important assets I have to offer are my passion for the work you exhibit, a willingness to work hard and a desire to contribute in any way I can, to your winning team.

I would very much appreciate the opportunity to discuss the internship with yourself or a member of your team and would be happy to attend a meeting at the Gallery at your convenience.

I look forward to hearing from you.
Yours sincerely,

Simona Bartini

WORK PLACEMENT

From: Joe Cooper [mailto:joe_cooper@ucreative.webmail]

To: d_tracy@bskyb.webmail

Subject: Work Placement

FOR THE ATTENTION OF:
David Tracy,
Executive Producer of Rugby Union,
Sky Sports,
BSkyB

Dear Mr Tracy

I am writing to enquire about a work placement with Sky Sports
Rugby Union Department and hope you will consider me for this
opportunity. Sky Sports' comprehensive coverage of domestic,
international and southern hemisphere rugby union is second to
none. As a journalism student and passionate rugby fan I would
very much like to learn from individuals at the forefront of this
excellence.

In June this year, I expect to graduate with a BA Honours in
Journalism from the University for the Creative Arts and my
ambition is to become a sports journalist. Playing and watching
rugby forms a dominant part of my life. Before moving to
university I played county and divisional rugby in the South
East. Since then I have been a member of the Harlequins U19s and
U21s and this season I also captained my university's 1st XV and
represented English Universities.

I have good written and verbal skills and have written journalism
experience as Sports Correspondent for UCA's student newspaper; I
am also currently working as a trainee with a commercial radio
station in Surrey.

I can be available for a placement any time during March and
April and would be happy to attend an interview at any time
convenient to you. Please find attached a copy of my C.V. Thank
you for your time.

Yours sincerely,

Joe Cooper

3rd Year BA (Hons)
Journalism
07777 123456

CREATING AN IMPRESSION

PHILIP WYATT
UNIVERSITY
COLLEGE
FALMOUTH

CREATING AN IMPRESSION

By Jon Christie – Head of Careers, **University College Falmouth**

Whilst spending time creating the right look and feel for your CV, it is worth taking it one step further and incorporating your design into all your other business-facing products – covering letter, business cards, online portfolio, showreel and website, etc. In this way you are creating your own personal brand, which will help you to portray your professional persona. Branding can be done very simply by using consistent fonts, colours, spacing, images and possibly even a logo. Linking all the elements of your marketing products can, if done well, leave a strong and lasting impression with an employer or client.

You need to approach your personal branding just as you would any other design project where the overall impression is as important as the content. Remember marketing and branding are all about communication, so consider what it is you want to convey to your audience. What are your key qualities? What is your area of business? What are your unique selling points (USPs)? Your brand should reflect, or be sympathetic to, all of these facets, whilst creating a clear and consistent style.

We all communicate in different ways and at different levels depending on whom we are addressing. Ensure your marketing material is giving the right message, in the right way, to the right people. Before launching it, carry out some market research and get feedback from a mix of audiences. Take a closer look at the way famous brands market themselves – their packaging, their websites, their advertisements and even where they choose to advertise their products. All of this will help you to understand the subtle but powerful messages that can be conveyed through careful branding.

Attention to detail and the effects of those details on the final product all need to be examined carefully. The quality, weight and colour of paper can make an enormous difference to the impact you make. Using a slightly non-standard paper such as textured or off-white for your stationery can really make you stand out from the competition. Quality printing is equally important. Use a good printer you can trust or get it done professionally.

Make sure the effect you are trying to create is conducive to the way you send your branded information. How you dispatch your package – by post, in person or via email – can either contribute to, or detract from, the professional image you are trying to convey. Obviously if coloured or textured paper is part of the effect, then there is little point in sending your package by email.

Finally, ensure that you are portraying a consistent message that is reflected not only in your stationery but in the work you do, the way you write (your CV, cover letter or email) and the way your work is displayed. Any discrepancy and your brand will loose credibility.

EXPERT OPINION

Michael Smith

“ If we advertise a job then I definitely want to see a CV and a letter, and a folio of work. We see ourselves as communicators and we want to employ people who are good communicators. We judge the whole package, especially from students who, by necessity, don't have a particularly broad range of work.”

Michael Smith – Managing Director, **Cog Design**

SHOWING YOUR WORK

INTRODUCTION

By **Hilaire Graham** – Dean, Learning and Teaching, **University for the Creative Arts**

Whether you are sending your CV in response to a job advertisement or simply making initial contact with a prospective employer, it follows that you may want to attach material that shows your work. The form of this attachment may vary and choosing the most appropriate examples for each application is critical. Your material may be prints of images or files on a DVD or, as a creative practitioner, you may include a reference to your own website.

ATTACHING PRINTED EXAMPLES

Attaching pages of images is a quick and direct way to attract attention. Start by making a selection of the images most likely to intrigue the recipient. Make sure your examples provide strong evidence of the points you are trying to emphasise – your talents (such as drawing), your creativity (shown in your designs), or your proficiency in a particular skill (such as project development).

Do not try to show everything that you can do. Keep attached printed material to 2 x A4 sheets, so that the prospective employer can quickly gain an impression of your ability. The printed material needs to complement the information in your CV.

Make sure your images have clear titles that identify what they are, such as 'bus shelter design', or indicate the type of image, e.g. 'plan' or 'final design' etc. In designing your pages, think about the balance between text/image and white page.

Remember to test print before you send: the colour resolution onscreen is often different to the printed image and the print may look darker than you really want.

SENDING A DVD

Sending a DVD with a CV gives you the opportunity to send more visual information. You need to brand the DVD so that it is clearly labelled and links to your CV. In a busy office, it is very easy for them to become separated. Your branding on the DVD cover should be striking and intriguing and demand attention.

The DVD itself is fraught with difficulties. Busy employers might find loading a DVD and looking through files time-consuming. As with sending a CV electronically, there are often problems in opening files with different software versions or the prospective employer may not use the same program. Think about saving your work in accessible files, such as PDF format, but be aware that it may change the way your work can be shown.

Make sure you refer to projects in the CV and in your DVD file consistently so that the prospective employer can move seamlessly from one to the other.

SHOWREELS

A showreel provides a taster of your film or animation talents. Although you will have a showreel from your coursework, it should also include any commercial work you have completed as well as work undertaken in your own time. As with DVDs, make sure it can be clearly identified as yours.

You will need to think about the best way to get an employer to view your showreel e.g. on a DVD or online. There are pros and cons of each and many media professionals use both.

SHOWREELS

An advantage of sending a DVD is that you can tailor it to the needs and interests of the employer or client. Consider the skills you are demonstrating: is it your camera work, your storytelling or your editing? Think also about who is viewing the showreel and choose relevant material. If you are applying for a job with a company specialising in making music videos, a showreel depicting documentary film is unlikely to impress!

Choose only your very best pieces – quality is far more important than quantity. Start with your best piece to capture the interest of the viewer and finish with something that will leave a positive and lasting impression.

Categorise your work and provide a simple menu so that viewers can move easily from one section to another. Start each film with a short introduction, giving some basic but relevant information about the piece. As well as short packages of film you may also include stills and a CV on your DVD, which should all be easily accessible from the main menu.

In contrast, an online showreel will inevitably cover a wider range of material but has the advantage of immediacy.

Tamsin Baker has included her showreel on her website and tells the viewer that it takes two minutes to view (which is better than wondering when it is going to end and whether they have time to view it now).

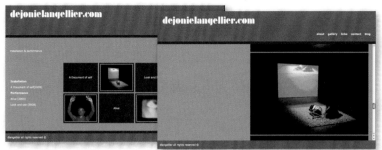

DEJONIE LANGELLIER
UNIVERSITY FOR THE CREATIVE ARTS

WEBSITES

Using the internet to create your own website is an effective way of enabling a prospective employer to view your work. As it will be available at all times and for all to see, there is always the chance that some influential person may stumble across your site. Because it is your website, you control what is available to view and you are responsible for maintaining and keeping it up to date with your achievements. You might refer to your website as an e-portfolio or an online portfolio, but it will be distinctively different to the paper-based portfolio that you might take to an interview.

Firstly, your website offers the prospective employer the opportunity to see your work at the time that they receive your job application or introductory letter. It may well be the convincing reason to invite you for an interview.

Secondly, it allows you to create opportunities for the viewer to select what they would like to see. It will not be simply sequential as is a paper-based portfolio, so you will need to ensure the site is reliable and easy to navigate.

Thirdly, it should include all the information that you have created about yourself, including your CV. A prospective employer may want to access a downloadable copy.

You will need to design your website thoughtfully. It should be part of the branding that you use for other information.

You can keep adding images of projects and other achievements to your website to keep it current. Remember when designing your site that it needs to last for at least a year; so try not to change it every other day or month. Prospective employers may want to go back to a site that they remember! Set a point in the future when you will refresh its look and review all your material. You may also have received some feedback on your website and CV that will help you evaluate how your look is working. If you are updating your site, it is useful to put a notice on the site letting visitors know when it will be back.

Be careful about the information that you give out over the internet: give the email address and phone number that are on your business card. Don't give out personal information such as your home address even if it is your business address currently. If arranging a meeting it might be useful to go to the enquirer's workplace or meet at a neutral venue such as a hotel or café until you have found out more about them.

ONLINE PORTFOLIOS

Some professional websites give you the opportunity to create an online portfolio on their website. For example the Chartered Society of Designers has a section of their site called 'Designer Select' for members to display details of themselves and their work.

BLOGGING

Using a blogging website enables you to represent yourself and your work very personally. This may be more appropriate to some disciplines than others. Remember that employers are looking at blogs and social networking sites to find out about you so make sure your sites are work-friendly.

You may use the blog as a diary or to invite comments and discussion about your work. You should think about how a blog can work to complement a website or online portfolio and provide a different view of you and your work.

BLOGGING
(CONT.)

Rosie Upright has created a blog that becomes a journey for the viewer. Images show her work in progress and other things that intrigue her from her surroundings. Rosie is able to invite comments from viewers to discuss her work.

CHECKLIST FOR CREATING AN ONLINE PORTFOLIO

✔ Your domain name should be memorable but professional. Use your own name, your company name or your brand name.

✔ Find a webhosting site that allows you to register and purchase domain names and web space. You will need to consider how much web space you will need and whether you can increase space at a later date.

✔ Make sure you choose a hosting site that is reliable.

✔ You will need to pay a monthly fee for web hosting and an annual fee for your domain name.

✔ The website design should reflect the design of your CV, business card and other information to create a professional appearance.

✔ Your website needs to be consistent in appearance and be easy for others to navigate.

✔ Test your site on different browsers: Mac and PC interfaces can work differently.

✔ Plan your website/online portfolio on paper initially, then start designing on the computer.

✔ Use specialist design software to design your site before you use the web software.

✔ Design the pages of your site to balance images and text.

✔ Design your site for SVGA screens (800 x 600 pixels, 15 x 17 inches).

EXPERT OPINION

Michael Smith

❝ My view on websites is to only tackle them if you are going to do it well. A badly designed site will let you down in the same way that badly mounted work will at an interview. I'd much rather see a great PDF of work, or a series of A4 print-outs, sent in the post.❞

Michael Smith – Managing Director, **Cog Design**

REVIEWING PROGRESS

INTRODUCTION

It is a good idea to take a step back, from time to time, to review your CV and job search strategies. How successful have you been in getting job interviews? If you have been sending out your CV but getting little or no response, then it is time to reassess your tactics.

Remember that rejection is a normal part of the job-seeking process and there can be many reasons for not getting an interview in a competitive job market.

Start by going back to the checklist on page 17 and look critically at your application. Perhaps a fresh pair of eyes is needed. Who do you know who could give you effective feedback? Most university careers services provide this service for recent graduates.

Have you applied for a job recently and wondered why you were not called for an interview? If you met the criteria for the job, feel you made a good application and have received an 'encouraging' rejection letter, then why not request further feedback? What harm can it do? At worst, you may not get a response but you should simply take that on the chin!

POSITIVE OUTCOMES

If you get as far as the interview but fail to get the job itself, then certainly ask for feedback. As long as you are polite and not too pushy, it will only go to show your genuine interest in the company and your eagerness to improve your application. Make a note of the names of the people you have met, write them a thank you note for giving up their time to see you and ask if they know of any future vacancies within their own or other organisations. The example email on page 56 encompasses all these features.

UNDERSTANDING THE GRADUATE JOB MARKET

Many job opportunities are never advertised publicly. Positions are often filled internally, by applicants already known to the organisation, or by being placed on closed sites and with employment agencies. So be proactive in your job search by using a wide range of strategies to promote yourself to potential employers. Use the checklist below to ensure your creative job search is broad and comprehensive. Remember you are unique with distinctive skills and abilities. **BELIEVE IN YOURSELF!**

CHECKLIST

- ✔ Seek out opportunities to meet and network with potential employers (e.g. seminars, shows, exhibitions).
- ✔ Sign up to receive networking emails and newsletters linked to your industry.
- ✔ Use your personal networks – family, friends and acquaintances – to look out for opportunities.
- ✔ Read industry-focused journals and newspapers to keep abreast of events within your field.
- ✔ Maintain contact with other graduates from your course; provide moral and practical support to each other.
- ✔ Check your university careers websites regularly.
- ✔ Check company websites for news and vacancies.
- ✔ Look out for company open days/visits.
- ✔ Telephone selected employers to find out about the industry.
- ✔ Arrange to meet or shadow someone who is doing the type of job you are seeking.
- ✔ Consider volunteering or doing work experience to keep your skills current.
- ✔ Consider seeking a temporary or lower level job within the industry.
- ✔ Register with recruitment agencies.
- ✔ Join a professional association.
- ✔ Find a mentor who will provide you with moral support.
- ✔ Seek a second opinion on your CV and job applications.
- ✔ Review your skills portfolio. Do you need to undertake any short courses to update or add to your skills?
- ✔ Request feedback from companies following unsuccessful applications.

REQUESTING FEEDBACK

From: Jon Andrews [mailto:jonandrews@webmail.co.uk]

To: gareth@abcorganisation.co.uk

Subject: Job Vacancy – New Graduate (407)

Dear Gareth

I have just received the email with news of my unsuccessful application (I hope you do not mind my emailing you directly about this). Firstly, thank you very much indeed for your time in considering my application. Whilst I am obviously disappointed, I understand that the standard of the other applicants was high.

I was wondering if you could give me a little more detail in your feedback? This is absolutely the area that I am looking to work in and feel that my skills and education would most benefit. It was clear that "experience" was an area I was lacking but, as this position was aimed at new graduates, I think many applicants were also weak in this area; is there anything specifically that you feel may benefit me in future applications?

The email from your HR Department recommended I apply for similar positions both within your Company and elsewhere. From your experience and knowledge, are there any organisations/institutions that may be looking to recruit for a similar role?

You mentioned there was a remote possibility that you may add to the team in the future and I will keep a keen eye out for any advertising of that post.

Thanks again for your time and good luck with everything

Jon

Jon Andrews
07777 123456